LIBRARY/

3 ⟨ **S0-BRY-733**

HD 69 .P75 A285 2009

9

97 things every project manager
should know

Every Project

DATE DUE

			PRINTED IN U.S.A.

NEW ENGLAND INSTITUTE OF TECHNOLOGY.
LIBRARY

97 Things

Every Project Manager Should Know

Collective Wisdom from the Experts

Edited by Barbee Davis

NEW ENGLAND INSTITUTE OF TECHNOLOGY
LIBRARY

O'REILLY®

Beijing · Cambridge · Farnham · Köln · Sebastopol · Taipei · Tokyo

1-15

#4397 49645

97 Things Every Project Manager Should Know
Edited by Barbee Davis

Copyright © 2009 Barbee Davis. All rights reserved.
Printed in the United States of America.

Published by O'Reilly Media, Inc. 1005 Gravenstein Highway North, Sebastopol CA 95472

O'Reilly books may be purchased for educational, business, or sales promotional use. Online editions are also available for most titles (*http://my.safaribooksonline.com*). For more information, contact our corporate/institutional sales department: (800) 998-9938 or *corporate@oreilly. com*.

Editor: Mike Loukides

Series Editor: Richard Monson-Haefel

Production Editor: Rachel Monaghan

Proofreader: Rachel Monaghan

Compositor: Ron Bilodeau

Indexer: Julie Hawks

Interior Designer: Ron Bilodeau

Cover Designer: Mark Paglietti

Print History:

August 2009:   First Edition.

The O'Reilly logo is a registered trademark of O'Reilly Media, Inc. *97 Things Every Project Manager Should Know* and related trade dress are trademarks of O'Reilly Media, Inc.

PMP is a registered certification mark, PgMP is a registered service mark, and PMBOK is a registered trademark of the Project Management Institute, Inc.

Many of the designations used by manufacturers and sellers to distinguish their products are clarified as trademarks. Where those designations appear in this book, and O'Reilly Media, Inc. was aware of a trademark claim, the designations have been printed in caps or initial caps.

While every precaution has been taken in the preparation of this book, the publisher and authors assume no responsibility for errors and omissions, or for damages resulting from the use of the information contained herein.

RepKover. This book uses Repkover,™ a durable and flexible lay-flat binding.

ISBN: 978-0-596-80416-9

[M]

Contents

Tips by Topic

Agile Methods

Software Development

Managing People and Teams

International Issues or Distributed Teams

Managing Projects

Communications

Managing Stakeholders

Project Processes

Project Requirements

End-Users

Purchasing Issues

Self-Management

Web Development

Preface

IN THEORY, CREATING A NEW PRODUCT or introducing a new process is simple. In reality, those of us who actually do it for a living know that it is becoming increasingly chaotic.

97 Things Every Project Manager Should Know is a collection of wisdom from project managers, software developers, and a wide range of other occupation holders from all around the world who are successful in managing their teams to success. They have shared what they think are important tips for you to know, whether you are involved in trying to create the product or manage the processes of your organization's projects.

Traditional books teach theory. In this one, people who are actively working in the field day to day share the best secrets that they have learned or developed after years on the job. You can find practical suggestions to improve both the final product and your personal experiences by taming the chaos and guiding the project to a successful completion.

As I talk to active practitioners, I find that there is a growing trend to involve software developers, research chemists, construction foremen, and all manner of other industry-specific technical experts in projects in a more vocal and active way. Users, and other stakeholders, must also be included in this ever-more-democratic vocation. While this cooperation is great, it multiplies the complexity of trying to get the work finished.

Interestingly, when editing this book I have found that regardless of industry, project role, or worldwide location, those of us who have project responsibilities face the same challenges. And the joy has been that these tip authors from around the world have been willing to share their ideas to help us master those challenges. Since they represent not only project managers, but the voices of those new technical stakeholders in the project, this is your chance to hear their ideas and concerns before facing similar participants in your workplace.

Based on my firm belief that shared knowledge is power, this book was created by combining the work of authors from 29 United States locations and 12 other countries around the world. The authors have donated their thoughts and advice to help others in the field grow and prosper through more skillful project guidance. It is a testament to the intensity of today's belief in the value of a collaborative environment that, despite wrestling with their own daily issues, these authors were still willing to take the time to help us all benefit from their wise, field-tested solutions.

Permissions

The licensing of each tip is similar to open source. Every contribution is available online and licensed under Creative Commons, Attribution 3, which means that you can use the individual contributions in your own work as long as you give credit to the original author. Other open source books have been tried and have, with only a few exceptions, failed. I believe that is because it's harder for individuals to contribute to a project unless it can be modularized. This book succeeds for exactly that reason: each contribution is self-contained and works both in this larger collection and on its own.

How to Contact Us

Please address comments and questions concerning this book to the publisher:

> O'Reilly Media, Inc.
> 1005 Gravenstein Highway North
> Sebastopol, CA 95472
> 800-998-9938 (in the United States or Canada)
> 707-829-0515 (international or local)
> 707-829-0104 (fax)

On the web page for this book, we list errata and any additional information. You can access this page at:

> *http://www.oreilly.com/catalog/9780596804169/*

To comment or ask technical questions about this book, send email to:

> *bookquestions@oreilly.com*

For more information about our books, conferences, Resource Centers, and the O'Reilly Network, see our website at:

> *http://www.oreilly.com/*

Safari® Books Online

 When you see a Safari® Books Online icon on the cover of your favorite technology book, that means the book is available online through the O'Reilly Network Safari Bookshelf.

Safari offers a solution that's better than e-books. It's a virtual library that lets you easily search thousands of top tech books, cut and paste code samples, download chapters, and find quick answers when you need the most accurate, current information. Try it for free at *http://my.safaribooksonline.com*.

Acknowledgments

The idea for *97 Things Every Project Manager Should Know* was not conceived in a vacuum. There are many people who deserve credit for the concept and its execution.

I would like to thank the series editor, Richard Monson-Haefel, whom I met while helping to administrate the No Fluff Just Stuff symposiums for Jay Zimmerman. After finding out about my focus on project management and software development, he suggested I write a book for his "97 Things" series called *97 Things Every Project Manager Should Know* as a companion piece for his own book, *97 Things Every Software Architect Should Know*.

A public wiki was created on the O'Reilly Media website, so that everyone around the world who wished to participate could be involved. I'm deeply grateful to those who chose to donate their time and contribute tips to this book.

O'Reilly deserves credit for listening to this idea with open ears, and backing what is more or less an untested method of creating a book. O'Reilly also merits praise for agreeing that all content will be open source (Creative Commons, Attribution 3). The people at O'Reilly I would specifically like to thank include Mike Loukides, Rachel Monaghan, Ed Stephenson, and Laurel Ackerman. Without your help and guidance, this project would not have been possible.

O'Reilly is developing other "97 Things" titles. The idea is to create a new and unique series that leverages the collaborative intelligence and practical experience of experts in every field. Project management, software development, and data architecture are just a few of the topics we are already pursuing.

Get Users Involved As Early As Possible

Barbee Davis, MA, PHR, PMP
Omaha, Nebraska, U.S.

PAST PATTERNS OF SOFTWARE DEVELOPMENT involved getting user requirements and then going off to do the coding and testing under a veil of great secrecy. After all, the users wouldn't understand what we were doing anyway, right? At the end of the project, our magician's magic cloth was whisked away and the user was expected to "ooh" and "ahh" at the brilliance of what we had produced. However, all too frequently the reaction was, "Well, I know you went to a lot of work, but what I really wanted was…."

Today, the secret to project success is to involve the users almost as soon as there is anything visible to show them. How much better it is to find out that there are problems with what we are developing early on, rather than after the project is complete!

Costs for changes become increasingly high the further along we are on the project schedule timeline. The time to recode, retest, and rework the immediate software, as well as to test integration with all the peripheral code involved, can delay the project substantially. And both time and cost baselines are jeopardized if a change is so major that it has to go through a lengthy Change Control Board process for approval.

Programming decisions over very minor issues, which make perfect sense to the software developer and the project manager, may create chaos back at the workstation when the software goes into use.

I know of a large training company that spent $5 million redesigning its ordering software. Previously, the item numbers matched the product being ordered in a logical way. For example, 4125 might be a student manual, 4225 was the accompanying student exercise disk, 4325 could represent the instructor manual, 4425 was the course outline for marketing purposes, and so on. You could order all the items in the 4X25 series on the same screen.

Each day, administrative coordinators in 140 locations around the world ordered the same kinds of materials over and over and soon memorized the item numbers. Once you knew the number for a student manual, you could immediately key in the numbers for the other items without looking them up, and ordering went quickly.

In the redesign, somehow the project team forgot to consider the way the ordering process was used by the real people doing it. Under the new design, there was no logical relationship between items. Item 6358 might be the same student manual that once was 4125, the accompanying student exercise disk was now 8872, and the instructor manual for the same class was 3392.

Not only did the user have to look up each item and try to "forget" the old numbers and system, but also each type of item was now on a separate page.

Administrative coordinators were furious. Ordering slowed to a crawl. The project far exceeded its time and cost baselines.

As a project manager, you should get the users talking to the software developers early and often.

Avoid Whack-a-Mole Development

Venkat Subramaniam
Broomfield, Colorado, U.S.

SOFTWARE PROJECT MANAGERS face a lot of pressure to deliver fast. Time is of the essence. How can you get things done fast?

Imagine you have two programmers on your team, Bernie and Rob. Both are capable, have the same amount of domain knowledge, and have equal language skills. During development, you find that Bernie finishes his feature implementations much faster than Rob.

While Bernie focuses on getting the code completed quickly, Rob spends time writing code and then refactoring* it. He names the variables and methods better. Once he gets things working, he breaks the code into smaller pieces. Now he writes tests to make sure each piece of his code does what he meant it to do. When he's reasonably satisfied, he declares the coding of that functionality done.

But assume you don't know these details. If you only look at the speed with which the functionalities are declared done, clearly Bernie is the better man, right?

A few weeks go by, and you demonstrate the features to your customer. As usual, the customer loves your completed features, but now wants you to change and improve them. You ask your developers to make those code alterations. When you take the new and improved functionality back to your customer, they try out the features that Rob implemented and are pleased with the changes.

---

* *Refactoring*: Reworking the body of code to improve its internal structure without changing its external function. It improves the software design. Refactoring code is going back to improve a working feature that was created quickly and tested. Now it needs further internal refinement to facilitate its long term use and make it easier to add future changes.

Unfortunately, they discover something odd with the features that Bernie implemented. While Bernie has programmed in the new functions fine, now a few things that worked before don't work anymore. The customer marks these as defects, and you ask Bernie to fix them. The customer tests the features again. Now even newer, stranger things seem to be broken. What's going on here?

If you have a child, you know what is happening. Bernie has created a Whack-A-Mole application. Whack-A-Mole is a toy. Kids are given a wooden hammer to strike moles that pop up at random. It's fun for them to be surprised by which mole pops up next. However, fixing applications with broken code popping up at random places is not fun. It is frustrating, unpredictable, and it slows your product development. Bernie was sprinting initially, but he was running in the wrong direction.

While Rob appeared slower at the outset, he was actually creating superior code. His pace proved sustainable. The better quality of his initial code helped him make workable changes quickly. Plus, the tests he wrote in the beginning gave him instant feedback regarding whether or not his new code was compatible with other parts of the application where the code was used.

When measuring time for a feature implementation, do not consider only the time it takes to write it in the first place. Add the time it takes to enhance, fix, and improve the code. Writing good quality code and tests takes time. It appears to be a short-term loss. However, it comes with a long-term gain.

Ask yourself if you want speed, or if you want to savor sustainable progress.

A Word Can Make You Miss Your Deadline

Pavel Simsa, PMP
Bellevue, Washington, U.S.

WHICH WORD CAN MAKE YOU MISS YOUR DEADLINE? The answer is "any word." When you are developing a product that will be released in languages other than English, you are adding numerous new risks and constraints to your project.

Some are technical and obvious. For example, if your product will be released in Japanese, it has to support the appropriate fonts. If it doesn't, the Japanese version won't work, even if the English one works perfectly. But font compatibility is not under your control. You and your team need to be aware of translation quirks and consider them before coding. Make sure that the development practices follow international standards that will eliminate such issues.

However, the mere need for alternate language versions also constrains what decisions you can make and when. Typically, localization (Japanese, Swedish, German, etc.) happens in parallel with English development, with a certain lag. It can be a few days, weeks, or even months. However, at some point the translation of the foreign version has to "catch up" with the English version.

You need to make sure during testing and reviews that:

- What is in the English version can be properly translated
- What is translated truly corresponds to the English version
- The translated product works flawlessly

Here's the catch. These three things may be tested after the English version is finished and signed off on. During the testing and reviewing of a localized version, you will always find at least one challenging issue that can't be solved except through a change to the English product.

However, be aware that a relatively simple and low-risk last-minute change in the English product, such as rephrasing a sentence (which takes only a few seconds to code), often requires several days to implement and retest for all the localized versions.

This can cost thousands of extra dollars, especially if you are contracting the translation work to an external company. The mistake that less experienced software development project managers often make is simple. They underestimate the effect and magnitude of making unexpected changes to the English version.

Here are two main things you can do to prevent this:

- Add a "localization buffer" to the end of your schedule. *End of schedule* means the effective deadline for any work on the English product included in your project schedule. Any changes that need to be done after that targeted end date must meet very specific and very strict criteria to "get in" to the rework queue. Every change to this version also necessitates changes to the foreign ones.

- Sequence the tasks in a way that quality control of functionality is done separately from quality review of the English text. That can be as simple as copying all of the English text to a spreadsheet for proofing. That way, unclear wording can be found before the test cycle reveals it on an otherwise functioning product. Now, the necessary change can be done earlier and may not necessitate reworking other language versions.

Make Project Sponsors Write Their Own Requirements

Miyoko Takeya, PMP
Tokyo, Japan

PROJECT FAILURE IS NOT JUST A PROBLEM with American corporations. According to a survey conducted several years ago by one of Japan's leading information technology magazines, more than 75% of the projects that are undertaken by Japanese corporations are considered a failure when measured against the metrics of quality, cost, and delivery.

In Japan, as in most other nations, the top reason for failure in each metric is almost always the same: *poor requirements definition*. The companies that are most at risk are those with poor business analysis capabilities. When specifically reporting on technology projects, such as software development, success is categorized, euphemistically, as "improbable." This result shows how difficult it is to find, identify, and define true requirements for a software project.

Since it is so hard to do, many project owners—such as customers, project sponsors, or company executives—expect the project manager to define and refine the requirements for the software on her own. They do not provide much in the way of guidance or a clear definition of what they need. Since it is a software project, and they may not understand software development themselves, they assume that they don't have to define what they expect.

The software project manager usually does not have the authority or the time to find, select, and prioritize the project requirements on her own—especially since there may be several interest groups involved in the project that probably have conflicting ideas about what they envision the software will do upon completion.

It's up to the project manager to spend time with those who are funding the software project to help them define exactly what they want before the project starts. Is it more important that it is done quickly, with few bugs, or on as small a budget as possible? You can't have it all. What resources and skill sets are crucial to create the software they want? Are they making these resources available to the team?

How will the software be used to run the infrastructure or make money for the company? Are the time constraints realistic? Are they written into a customer contract, tied to an important holiday date, or part of an elaborate marketing plan?

Without serious, specific consideration of what is to be created on this project during the requirement definition phase, the success of the project is severely jeopardized. Remember, project owners need to convey what they want this software to do, not how the programmers will go about producing that result.

Convince the project owners that they must be involved in the process from start to finish. Solid requirements planning establishes a clear connection between the business case, project goals, and the project outcome. Otherwise, the project cannot produce the satisfactory result they are expecting.

A failed software project hurts the project owners most, since they have put up the money to fund the project and were expecting to use the software to earn back their investment.

Favor the Simple Over the Complex

Scott Davis
Broomfield, Colorado, U.S.

AS FAR AS I'M CONCERNED, my microwave oven only has one button: "add a minute." To boil a cup of water for my coffee, I press the button three times. To melt cheese on my crackers, one click. To warm up a flour tortilla, I press "add a minute" and then open the door after 15 seconds.

Would a one-button microwave oven ever make it out of the planning committee? Probably not. I can tell by the (never used) features on my microwave that the committee favored complexity over simplicity. Of course, they probably cloaked "complexity" in the euphemism "feature-rich." No one ever starts out with the goal of making a product that is unnecessarily complex. The complexity comes along accidentally.

Suppose that I have a slice of cold pizza that I want to warm up. According to the manufacturer's directions, I should press the "menu" button. I am now faced with the options "speedcook" or "reheat." (Um, "reheat," I guess, although I'm kind of hungry. I wonder if speedcook will be any faster than reheat?)

"Beverage," "pasta," "pizza," "plate of food," "sauce," or "soup"? (I choose "pizza," although it does have sauce on it, and it is on a plate.) "Deli/Fresh" or "Frozen"? (Neither, actually—it's leftover delivery pizza. I'll choose "Deli/Fresh," I guess.) "1 slice," "2 slices," "3 slices," or "4 slices"? I have no idea how much longer this interrogation will last, so I press Cancel and then the "add a minute" button.

What does this have to do with software development? As far as I'm concerned, Amazon.com only has one button: "one-click purchase." Oh, sure, I had to type in my address and my credit card number the first time I visited, but now I am one click away from my impulse buy.

Software generally solves complex problems. The question is how much of that inherent complexity are you forcing onto the end-user? Is your software a complexity amplifier? Great software is generally a complexity sink—it bears the brunt of the problem on behalf of the user instead of passing it along.

As a software project manager, are you a complexity sink or a complexity amplifier? The best ones absorb complexity from all sides—from the programmers, from the end-users, from management—and never amplify it. As the end-users generate seemingly contradictory requirements, your job is to help clean them up, rather than passing them blindly on to the developers. As the developers cite arcane technical reasons for not being able to fulfill a requirement, your job is to translate (absorb) that complexity and present the end-users with enough information to help them choose a different path.

How easy is it to use your application? How easy is it to add a new feature to your application? How easy is it to request a new feature? Report a bug? Deploy a new version? Roll back a bad version?

Simplicity doesn't happen accidentally. It needs to be actively cultivated. Complexity is what happens when you aren't paying attention.

Pay Your Debts

Brian Sletten
Beverly Hills, California, U.S.

DEBT, WHEN WELL MANAGED, is a useful financial instrument for both ordinary citizens and successful organizations. It balances present insufficiencies by borrowing against future surpluses. Used judiciously, short-term debt is an effective tool for smoothing out the rough edges of cash ebbs and flows. When abused, it becomes a burdensome yoke that makes it increasingly stressful to move along.

In the world of software development, borrowing time can be a useful strategy for meeting "at risk" milestones, while completing most of what needs to be done. Ward Cunningham introduced the notion of "technical debt" as something developers can incur as they head toward the end of an iteration,* or a deadline, if time gets short. At that point, they may not be able to do code right, but by taking some shortcuts they may be able to program code "right enough" to still cross the finish line.

Even though the software is in a temporary, imperfect state, this is a perfectly reasonable thing to do if the technical debt incurred is managed responsibly. If it is not paid off, however, it will start to become more painful to do over time. Continued borrowing against the future without repayment will put the project further at risk.

The best way to pay off your technical debt is to assess what "loans" were taken at the end of each iteration. Ask your developers to identify specific hacks† they would like to unwind, and quantify how much time they think they need to do so.

---

* *Iteration*: A short period of time chosen by an agile project team (a week, two weeks, a month, etc.) during which a key requirement chosen by the customer will be developed, tested, and then delivered to the customer for approval or comment. The next iteration will then begin to develop the next most important requirement and/or correct the work done in the preceding iteration.

† *Hack*: A quick fix or solution to a programming problem that works, but is less than ideal and may need to be revised when time allows. Fixing the inelegant code may be referred to as "unwinding a hack."

They do not need to pay debt off immediately, but it is good to gauge the extent of the needed repair while the shortcuts are still fresh in the developers' minds.

Make sure there are specific code problems identified to be rewritten, not just arbitrary buckets of time requested. This is not an opportunity to goof off, it is a disciplined approach to keeping your code base clean.

Additionally, an increasing array of software analysis tools such as code coverage, coupling analysis, and detection of style deviations can automatically help identify places where debt has been incurred, perhaps without your knowledge. Enter these items into your issue tracking system and schedule them against future iterations. By balancing the workload to include new business functionality and paying off loans, it is possible to keep your technical debt from spiraling out of control while still satisfying customer feature requests.

Software gets unwieldy for many reasons. But it usually comes down to hacks, insufficient documentation, inappropriate dependencies, shortcuts, and deviations from the intended design. When developers throw up their hands and say they need to start over on a system, chances are that unpaid technical debt has become overwhelming. They feel the need to declare the software equivalent of bankruptcy.

By identifying this debt along the way and dealing with it quickly, you can make more frequent "minimum payments" to prevent ensuing chaos. This metaphor is a surprisingly useful way to explain to business stakeholders how software can become unmanageable over time and why they should invest in keeping code clean.

Add Talents, Not Skills, to Your Team

Richard Sheridan
Ann Arbor, Michigan, U.S.

I USED TO HIRE THE WAY EVERYONE IN OUR INDUSTRY HIRED: skills, skills, skills. One day an interview candidate threw cold water in my face, figuratively, and it changed me.

I was looking to add a new hero to my team, someone with years of Microsoft experience. Looking over Bill's resume, I could tell he was perfect for the position. He had over six years of experience in all the relevant skills. If I could hit the right price point, this was going to be easy.

Bill came in for the interview. We talked and I described the projects we had on tap, and what a perfect fit Bill was for this position. I was sure this was going well. Suddenly, I realized I wasn't going to get him. I stopped the interview in mid-stream and asked Bill what had happened. I told him he was perfect for the position, but that I sensed he wasn't coming.

His response was, "Rich, if I wanted to do what I've been doing the last six years, I'd stay where I am. I heard you had some cool, new Java projects coming up and I wanted to work here because I saw it as a chance to learn and grow."

That's when it dawned on me. Hiring by running a "resume versus skills" match is the stupidest way a manager could ever build a team.

You see, my partners and I got into the high-tech industry because we wanted to be at the leading edge of technology. None of us hoped to spend a career recycling the same skills we learned in college. We got into this game because it would always be about new frontiers and learning new techniques and technologies.

But somewhere along the way, things went horribly wrong. I realized we had stopped investing in our employees' growth. We weren't looking for fresh, new talent. We were looking for very specific, already refined, skills. Now, I tell people that if they see an employer hiring for an exact skill match, what that employer is really saying is, "We don't plan to invest in you."

My advice to anyone seeking to build a strong team is to hire for talents, not for skills. What talents do I look for when hiring technologists for my agile development teams? Good kindergarten skills:

- Do the candidates get along well with others?
- Do they play nice?
- Do they put their things away when they have finished playing?
- Are they excited about new things?
- Do they like learning?

I can teach skills. In fact, in our agile team environment, learning technology is fast and easy. However, it is nearly impossible to teach an adult how to play nice.

Hiring for talents, not for skills, is a radically different way to build a team. However, I want to work with those who are poised to move enthusiastically beside me into exciting, new future technology.

Keep It Simple, Simon

Krishna Kadali, M. Tech
Kondapur, Hyderabad, India

STAKEHOLDERS OF THE PROJECT often make things more complicated than they need to be. This a common cause of software project failures. The team members of the project must have the ability to completely visualize the objectives of the project and complete actual work. Stakeholders, however, can accomplish the project in several simple, magical steps in their own minds. They imagine achieving the end solution quickly and easily, no matter how complex it is.

Stakeholders should not build a software project as a monolithic, gigantic, inflexible monster; instead they should allow the information technology team to build it like an onion, with each layer enhancing its maturity. There is no other alternative in the world of reality. Regardless of the completeness of the requirements, there will always be change. If your software is not flexible enough to quickly adapt to changing requirements, the project is dead even before it has begun.

To keep things simple, following are the key points to keep in mind:

- **Keep the requirements simple.** The business analysts often confuse a particular solution that came to their mind with the actual customer requirement based on a business need. Although the real requirement may be something very simple, there may be a communications gap between business analysts and programmer/developers since neither really understands what the other does.

  Business analysts should write requirements using simple tree-based imagery. The root requirement is the simple objective of the overall project. Small twig sets of child-level requirements are grouped together to form a branch representing a parent-level requirement. This process is repeated on the diagram until each requirement is crystal-clear. Software mind-mapping tools could be used to document the requirements using this approach. Once even a small set of requirements is crystallized, development can begin.

- **Follow agile development processes.** As soon as a small set of requirements is identified, the development team can start prototyping immediately. Once the prototype is available, stakeholders can test and provide feedback. Customer feedback ensures that requirements are accurate and also helps identify any gaps that developed in the requirements as they were relayed from the actual customer, through the business analysts, to the project team. Allowing the customer to see the prototype also checks that the corresponding solution imagined by the developers is, indeed, what the customer envisioned.

  Gaps are translated into new requirements, developers re-prototype, and the cycle continues. Each cycle should be as short as possible—typically, not more than two to three weeks.

  This cycle of defining a small set of requirements, producing a prototype of the stated requirements, and obtaining feedback ensures that all project stakeholders are always on the same page and everyone is comfortable with what is going on. By religiously following these simple techniques, every software project can reach a successful conclusion. Especially if success is defined as a happy customer and working software that provides the useful business function for which it was created.

You Aren't Special

Jared Richardson
Morrisville, North Carolina, U.S.

REMEMBER WHAT YOUR MOM TOLD YOU? "You're special! You're unique!" Right, just like every other boy or girl who had a mom! Believing that loving lie leads to common software project problems.

I coach many different teams. Without fail, the teams who believe they're "special" are always behind when judged by how well they meet their software project metrics. Because they think they're special, they have a strong inclination to reinvent everything. They think, "No other team could have possibly developed usable software, or at least not as outstanding as what we create among ourselves." Instead of learning from the mistakes of other developer teams, they insist on making their own mistakes. Over and over and over. At company expense.

They spend so much time rewriting, debugging, and putting their own twist on software and tools* that are already industry standard that they never finish customer projects. The ones they should sell to people for money. Those mythical, magical products that would be as special as the team, if only it ever got them written.

To hear this unique group of developers tell it, there are no existing build systems that can handle their "one of a kind" requirements. So, they must write a new one for each new project. Instead of reusing an existing object-database mapping tool, they write their own. Web application framework? We can do that, they profess. Continuous integration? Check. Testing harnesses? Let's write those, too. The vainest and most disillusioned of them will even attempt to write their own programming languages.

---

* *Tools*: Simple programs that software developers use to create, debug, test, analyze, track, or otherwise support quality software development.

So how do these teams spend their day? Solving the problems they've created by substituting the untested code they built themselves for the fully functional software tools usually available to them for free. When they write their own database layer, they spend the days tracking down obscure performance bugs and caching issues. Handling the edge cases[†] ends up consuming more time than they ever would have spent learning, or even modifying, existing tools.

The reason less "special" (but more successful) teams use existing tools is because the problems they're setting out to solve are hard problems. They need reliable tools so their attention is focused on the solution to their software project, not on trying to refill an already brimming toolbox.

What does this have to do with effective software project management? Don't let your programmers reinvent the wheel. When they come to you explaining how special their problems are, point out that their mothers may have stretched things when they made that "you're special" assessment. Be knowledgeable about what's available and guide your team toward high-quality open source or commercial tools.

The "not invented here" syndrome derails so many great teams. Don't let it derail yours.

---

† *Edge case*: A problem or situation that only occurs at the extremes (for example, fastest or slowest speed, highest or lowest volume of data, or with the oldest or newest browser interface). Often it means focusing on trivial things that drain time while important programming throughput is ignored.

Scrolling Through Time

Kim MacCormack
Leesburg, Virginia, U.S.

TWELVE YEARS AGO, my team was hired to develop a web application as a subcontractor for a graphic design firm. We were to have no direct contact with the customer. All of the requirements were relayed by the client to our prime contractor, and then passed on to us in a series of random emails.

One email concerned the screen resolution our artists should use. The previous standard had been 640×480, but more current research suggested that the web site should support up to an 800×600 resolution. (Today the most common screen resolution is 1,024×768.) Even though this was an experienced design firm, its formal requirements (which we never saw) to the customer stated:

> The layout of each page will conform to a fixed 800-pixel width standard and 600-pixel height standard.

If we had seen this requirement, we would have immediately corrected the statement to read, "The layout of each page will conform to a fixed 800-pixel width standard, to support up to an 800×600 monitor resolution." Since we had worked on many websites, we knew that the most important dimension was the width. Users hate scrolling horizontally, while vertical scrolling is considered one of the realities, if not advantages, of using a browser. However, evidently this valuable truth was never conveyed to the customer.

The content this novice website customer provided for each web page was huge. As a result, very few pages could be completely viewed (lengthwise) on a 15-inch monitor set to an 800×600 resolution. One had to scroll vertically.

Not realizing we would have to be miracle workers to make this oversized content display on a single screen, the end-user customer got very upset. They blamed our prime contractor, the design shop. In return, the design shop refused to pay us. According to them, we "did not meet the requirements as written."

From that experience, I have learned the danger of poorly constructed, written requirements and how they can be used against you. It is important to always document your assumptions and insist on reviewing and signing off on requirements with the end-user, not just with a middleman.

Fortunately, agile project management practices have alleviated some of these issues. By recognizing the importance of nose-to-nose interfaces between the developer and the real customer, we have evolved to collectively creating User Stories, and prioritizing features based on the business value they will provide to the customer, rather than requirements lists. A one- or two-week iteration process means we have early and frequent feedback, and the opportunity to clarify customer expectations.

Twelve years later, I have run into almost exactly the same situation with a client who is highly concerned about vertical scrolling, even though he wants large amounts of content on the page. Luckily, with the way we run projects today and the lessons I learned from my past experience, we resolved this issue quickly and set realistic customer expectations without the chaos of the past.

Save Money on Your Issues

Randy Loomis, PMP
Andover, Connecticut, U.S.

OUR COMPANY WAS USING TRAINING SOFTWARE that was five upgrades behind. We reached the point where it was so out of date that the vendor would no longer support it. Our project consisted of working with the vendor to upgrade our training software to the latest release, and then to train our users to use the newest version.

We developed two statements of work, one that outlined the user training agreement and one that delineated a "not-to-exceed" cost for applying the upgrades to our old training software. After obtaining a copy of our data, the vendor began the process of remotely developing and testing the scripts* necessary to begin converting the data and applying the first of the upgrades.

Once the scripts passed vendor testing, they were migrated to our development environment where we performed user tests. This process was repeated as we added each of the five subsequent upgrades. While doing testing, we would document any issues that we encountered, then we retested those issues once the vendor had rewritten and retested their original scripts.

While working through each of the upgrades, the vendor's hours, multiplied by the billing rate established in the statement of work, were tracked against the "not-to-exceed" budget. As we progressed through the upgrades, we discovered bugs in the application upgrades themselves that were not related to the custom scripts written to install the upgrades. We thoroughly documented each issue, printing screens and providing step-by-step details of what we discovered, and how and where we encountered each issue.

---

* *Script*: In computer programming, a program or sequence of instructions that is carried out by a program rather than by the computer processor. Scripts can be used to control a software application without altering the core code of the application.

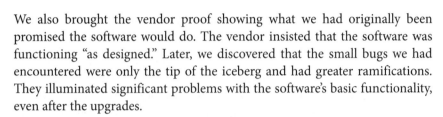

We also brought the vendor proof showing what we had originally been promised the software would do. The vendor insisted that the software was functioning "as designed." Later, we discovered that the small bugs we had encountered were only the tip of the iceberg and had greater ramifications. They illuminated significant problems with the software's basic functionality, even after the upgrades.

Over time, the vendor conceded that several of the issues we discovered were admittedly not "as designed"; rather, they were actual bugs. Remaining true to our "not-to-exceed" contract, our vendor did not charge us for the significant amount of work they were required to do to correct their own product after they reached the "not-to-exceed" total in our contract.

At this stage of the project, in order to meet critical deadlines, we were completely focused on getting the software installed. Our concern of whether an issue was "as designed" or a bug was the least of our worries. It became apparent that, had we been tracking vendor time specifically against each bug issue located, we might have avoided paying the "not-to-exceed" contract total cost.

When negotiating a contract with a vendor, specify that both the vendor's and your project team's time be tracked against each separate issue that is encountered. This will allow the software project manger to have an accurate record and be able to lower charges when there are issues with the vendor's original product, as opposed to problems with the contractual project work to implement it.

How to Spot a Good IT Developer

James Graham, PMP
Ta' l-Ibrag, Malta

SOFTWARE PROJECT MANAGERS know that project success rests on having excellent developers. How do you spot stellar performers in the applicant herd?

Before new candidates interview, talk to your best developers. Have them reaffirm the specific knowledge needed. Is experience with a particular development life cycle, a specific methodology, special toolsets, or definitive sector knowledge (experience in the defense industry or the pharmaceutical sector, for example) preferable, or mandatory?

Assess knowledge. Mix interviews, involving you and trusted representatives from your development team, with theoretical tests. A good software engineer will be able to fix "mock" syntax errors immediately and without any mental stress. He or she can read other people's code and understand its intent without extensive documentation or glyph-by-glyph translation. When presented with a programming problem, your candidate should be able to spot it and then describe it in both "developer geek" and in language appropriate for non-information technology stakeholders.

We all think "more is better" when hiring programming skills. But how do we define "more"? Although a candidate may have excellent knowledge, this person may not yet have developed the finesse to employ it effectively. A recent graduate or newly trained developer may struggle to apply the theoretical knowledge gained in an educational context when facing a demanding real-world project. When tight deadlines squeeze the time to explore solutions, and intense pressures from the client and other stakeholders loom, you need experience on top of raw knowledge.

Ask the applicant/developer to write code for review by you and your team. After analyzing the code and talking with your trusted developers, you will sense whether this person's approach and style will fit your team.

Consider the candidate's attitude toward work, coworkers, clients, and stakeholders. I once worked with a developer known as "The Hair Dryer." Legend has it that when he was upset, he could blow people's hair dry with his shouting. He was an excellent developer, but a detriment to a project team.

As the world moves toward agile development methodologies, cross-functional communication and soft skills will increase in importance. Developers will find themselves working in small teams with people from elsewhere in the organization. How well will your potential new teammate represent you when unleashed into the wild? Follow these simple guidelines when hiring software developers:

- Screen them to check for the right knowledge of development life cycles, methodologies, toolsets, and their industry/sector familiarity.

- Test them to see a demonstration of their ability to apply their knowledge in your workplace.

- Check out their communication and social skills.

- Look for the right attitude toward the work: a balance of desire to create high-grade products while accepting the project constraints. Is there documented evidence that they can produce products that are "fit for purpose," on time, and within the budget?

No matter how personable and skilled your applicant, always verify credentials with the issuing institutions and check out resume entries with former employers. Careful hiring practices may prevent a multitude of future problems.

Developer Productivity: Skilled Versus Average

Neal Ford
Atlanta, Georgia, U.S.

LET'S DEBUNK SOME OF THE MYTHS about developer skills for project managers who have been assigned for the first time to software projects. Understand that really good software developers are much more productive than average ones. In fact, some statistics say that really good developers are multiple orders of magnitude better than poor ones. One order of magnitude is the same as multiplying a quantity by 10. The point is, a skilled programmer isn't just a little better than an average one; the difference is huge.

What should this mean to our newly minted software project managers as they plan the development of this product? Managers erroneously think that even if you can't get the best and brightest, you still get some usefulness out of mediocre developers. But building software isn't like digging a ditch, where even the poorest ditch diggers can make a hole.

In software development, what is programmed today becomes the foundation for tomorrow. If you have mediocre developers building your foundation, the really good developers have to go back and fix the flaws before they can move on. Hiring mediocre or average developers slows project velocity.* Frequently, taking a poor performer off the team is more beneficial than adding a good one.

Couple this with the fact that adding people to a late project makes it even later, and you can understand why most enterprise development moves at a glacial pace. The nonexperienced software project manager might reason that if adding more warehouse men allows a truck to be loaded faster, hiring additional programmers would shorten the time necessary to complete a software project.

---

* *Velocity*: A term used in agile software development to show the rate of progress for a team or a team member, i.e., how much an individual programmer will be able to produce in a given time period.

That won't work. It will take time, and pull other programmers off-task, to get the new guys/gals up-to-date. In addition, the communication channels increase with each addition to the team. With a team of two, there is one channel: Betsy Sue to Bill. Add Mike, and you jump to three channels. The number of channels continues to grow exponentially.

Here's the formula: $n(n-1)/2$. With 12 people on the team, you have $12(12-1)/2$ channels, or 66 relationships you must maintain as the project manager. Add one more person, and you now have 78 communication channels to oversee.

Building software with average developers exposes two project myths: 1) that you can shorten a project by adding people, and 2) that it's OK to have average developers produce average (buggy/off-task) code at an average pace. In truth, average developers drag overall productivity down and the project takes longer than necessary to complete.

The solution? Give good developers powerful tools. You'll get higher-quality software faster. Second, having warm bodies doesn't help projects, and having to babysit poor developers cuts the productivity of your good developers, who are craftsmen. Software is too complex to turn into an assembly-line manufacturing process.

Want faster software development? Spend the extra money to hire and nurture excellent software developers. It will pay off in both the short term, and in the long term when it's time to maintain the code.

Size Matters

Anupam Kundu
New York, New York, U.S.

THE SIZE OF THE PROJECT, the size of the team, the size of the deliverables, and the size of the checklists—everything in a project depends on its SIZE. Size changes the rules of how the game is played.

The bigger the project gets (in size or complexity), the more important it becomes for a project manager to break down the project into manageable modules and share the delivery responsibility of these modules with capable people. This will ensure that key project members, including the project manager, can see the "big picture" without getting lost in the details while scouting for project health statistics.

Distributed projects tend to be bigger in size than other projects types; hence, the tactics the project manager uses to manage the size actually impacts the bottom line of the project. The word "big" conjures up a variety of images. It can mean anything from eight people working for 12 months (if you are a small vendor) to hundreds of people working on annual maintenance contracts (if you are an enormous IT partner for your client).

Here are a few suggestions on how to carve out the right size for the project and then make sure that everyone understands how the small parts of the puzzle can make or break the big picture:

- Break down the project into as many independent, yet manageable, workstreams as possible.

- Make sure each workstream has at least one key contact point responsible for its delivery.

- If possible, try to have key members play overlapping roles in these workstreams so that the "big picture" is shared across the teams.

- Track the progress (use any tool) of each workstream separately, and tie up the metrics at regular intervals to feel the pulse of the overall project.

- Document and share the risks, issues, assumptions, and dependencies of each workstream separately.

- Organize regular team meetings to share the status of each and every workstream.

- Publish an overall project roadmap, including release plans from all different workstreams.

- Use online tools aggressively to share user requirements, milestone updates, bug reports, report timelines, and risks.

For example, imagine you are entrusted with building three versions of the same website (North America, Asia-Pacific, and Mid-East). You decide it is best to create three different workstreams, each with an independent delivery contact person. Since all three sites are basically the same sites in a different version (leading to medium customization), have a few key resources float across all three workstreams. This way, they can ensure the overall integrity of the sites and suggest reuse of implementation details.

Another example might be that you have multiple integration vendors for a single project. It might be ideal to separate out each integration point (or a related collection of them) into an individual workstream. This will allow simultaneous channels of work and may shorten the delivery time. Involve the different teams in daily meetings to coordinate the overall quality of the delivery.

Document Your Process, Then Make Sure It Is Followed

Monte Davis, MCSE
Omaha, Nebraska, U.S.

DURING AN EMAIL MIGRATION FROM ONE PLATFORM TO ANOTHER, a woman got married and brought our email system to its knees.

The email flow works like this:

1. New emails coming in are delivered through the new email system.

2. If the new email system can, it delivers the message to the appropriate new system user. If not, the message is sent on to the old email system for delivery.

3. Emails sent *from* someone still on the old system *to* someone still on the old system are delivered to the appropriate mailbox. However, if the recipient has already been migrated to the new system, the email is automatically forwarded using a "migration" forwarding address created for each user.

Here's where the funny part comes in. Once Sally Single was migrated to the new email system, she had two email addresses, *sally.single@mycompany.com*, as well as a forwarding email address, *sally.single@migrate.mycompany.com*. All email sent to her from users on the old system would automatically be forwarded to the new mail system using her "migration" forwarding address.

When Sally got married and changed her name from "Sally Single" to "Sally Married," her email address changed as well. However, the person who renamed Sally's email address in the new system forgot to change her email "migration" forwarding address on the old system. So, Sally ended up with the following addresses.

New System	Old System
1. *sally.married@mycompany.com*	1. *sally.married@mycompany.com*
2. *sally.single@mycompany.com*	2. *sally.single@mycompany.com*
3. *sally.married@migrate.mycompany.com*	3. *sally.single@migrate.mycompany.com* (Original, unchanged migration entry that was overlooked after the wedding.)

When emails were sent to Sally from users still on the old messaging system, they created a loop: 1) Messages were created and sent on the old mail system to *sally.single@mycompany.com*; 2) old mail system checks Sally's account and sees that forwarding is set to *sally.single@migrate.mycompany.com* and forwards the messages; 3) the new mail system looks for someone with an email address equal to *sally.single@migrate.mycompany.com*, but it doesn't find it, since that address was renamed when Sally got married, so 4) the new mail system forwards the messages for the unknown recipient back to the old mail system; 5) the old mail system knows to forward all messages with an *@migrate.mycompany.com* address, so it forwards them to the new mail server; and 6) lather, rinse, repeat.

Every time the messages loop, the corporate legal disclaimer is added to the end of the messages. The legal disclaimer is only about 100 words, but when each message is looping between systems several times a minute, this adds up quickly. Evidently, Sally was very popular. There were so many messages sent to Sally that the size and volume of the messages brought the mail system to a grinding halt.

Moral of this story: document your processes and make sure the process is followed. Although the name change process had been documented, it was not being followed. Otherwise, Sally's user account on the old mail server would have been updated with her new, married name migration email address, and the issue would have been avoided.

Go Ahead, Throw That Practice Out

Naresh Jain
Malad, Mumbai, India

WHAT DO SUCCESSFUL TEAMS DO THAT OTHERS DON'T? They constantly question their own practices and try to eliminate wasteful ones. They mercilessly refactor their processes along with their software.

Il semble que la perfection soit atteinte non quand il n'y a plus rien à ajouter, mais quand il n'y a plus rien à retrancher. This French quote from Antoine de Saint Exupéry means "Perfection is attained, not when there is nothing more to add, but when there is nothing left to take away."

Why don't teams apply this principle today? Why is it that over a period of time, the value of the end product gets thinner and thinner, and the process and byproducts get bulkier and bulkier? Why do the lines of code expand, while the useful features of the software become fewer and fewer?

Key indicators that things are "broken" in the software development processes:

- The software bloats up in terms of lines of code and useless features
- The team building the software keeps growing in size
- The process gets more and more prescriptive, dogmatic, and rigid
- The team is experiencing "death by planning" meetings
- The amount of documents and supporting artifacts increases exponentially
- Newly discovered bugs keep pouring in from customer test groups

Team leaders have a tendency to keep adding more processes, more checks, and more audits, thinking that an increasingly stringent process will solve the problem. In my experience, it's never a process issue. Adding more processes will only make it that much more difficult for the team to see the root cause of the real problem.

Why is it that most teams are afraid to throw away practices that are not really helping the team? Why do teams start off with as many practices they can think of, instead of adding the practices just in time?

This could be a symptom of the team not really understanding why it is using the process in the first place. Or it could mean that someone who does not fully understand the software development process is forcing a heavy-handed methodology upon the team. In either case, the project becomes a "house of cards" ready to disintegrate into a useless pile of code bits. Trying to change anything, without understanding the true reason the project is expanding without adding value, is useless.

In my opinion, a good project manager should have a healthy grasp of how the team is working. He/she should be able to stand back and evaluate how each process imposed on the team impacts the throughput of functional software.

A knowledgeable project manager should sift through all the possible activities a team might be asked to do and retain only those that are vital to the success of this specific project. Once the leftover practices from projects past are swept away, the team's productivity and throughput should get better in a short period of time.

"Less is more" is a very important philosophy when it comes to process.

Requirement Specifications: An Oxymoron

Alan Greenblatt
Sudbury, Massachusetts, U.S.

GOOD REQUIREMENTS (R) describe how features of a product are going to solve particular existing or potential problems. Good features (F), sometimes called functionality, are added to products to address those important problems. Requirements are captured by salespeople or created by software project managers:

- We can't sell the product outside of the United States (R). We need to provide internationalization and location support (F).

- Users have to click five buttons to complete a very simple task. They get frustrated and never complete the task. We need to simplify the user interface (R) and reduce the number of button clicks to two or fewer to complete the same tasks (F).

Specifications (S), on the other hand, describe exactly how problems will be solved and the requirements will be met. Using the examples above, the following specifications might be written by systems architects:

- We will extract all text strings, including pop-up messages, and place them in external resource bundles (S).

- The application will be enhanced so that all text displayed on the screen will be retrieved from these resource bundles (S).

- Localization can be performed by creating specific resource bundles for the locales required (S).

- The functionality achieved through clicking buttons 1, 2, and 3 will be bundled into a single button click on Button A (S).

- The functionality of existing buttons 4 and 5 will be bundled into Button B (S).

Blurring the lines between requirements and specifications leads to the wrong people making the decisions. You either end up with the software developers making decisions about what features are important to a user, or with a software project manager telling a developer how to structure code. Either way, the result is a poor final software product.

Developers aren't usually out talking to customers, users, marketing, sales, and potential partners, trying to understand what new features are most important. On the other hand, software project managers usually aren't skilled developers who understand how best to implement a feature, and how their untrained, although well-meaning, specification suggestions would affect other aspects of the product. Each group has a unique skill set.

Having good requirements that describe the problem you are trying to solve, and why it is so important to solve this particular problem, lets the programmer be more flexible, efficient, and motivated during the development process. Coders can make independent design decisions as they work on the problem and understand it more thoroughly. They should only be bound by the technologies they have chosen to use, not by strict, brittle specifications created by a nonprogrammer.

Specifications still need to be written, but they will change. Have you come to the end of the product development cycle and only then fully understood how this product should have been built in the first place?

Keep the *what* you are trying to build separate from the *how* to build it. Then, let the properly trained team member make decisions based on his/her project role.

Success Is Always Measured in Business Value

Barbee Davis, MA, PHR, PMP
Omaha, Nebraska, U.S.

AS PROJECT MANAGERS, it's easy to get caught up in meeting our time, cost, scope, and quality baselines. The project quickly becomes an end in itself, and our personal worth becomes entwined with our ability to bring this project in according to these measurable expectations.

We need to focus on the fact that the project is only as successful as the business value it adds to the organization. If we're producing a software product for market, the evaluation factors for "success" are clear. We need to use our project management skills to bring this product to market quicker so we can get it sold to a large portion of the customer base before the competition is able to produce a similar or even better product.

We need to sell to a majority of the marketplace before the demand for this item dries up. We need to design this software so that it is easy for customers to install and learn to use. It needs to be easy to maintain and update.

Many software project managers feel their job is merely to get the software completed. Without connecting the project to the business need, great software could be a failure from the organization's return on investment (ROI) point of view.

If this is an internal project, how does this software project allow the organization to save or earn money? Will we need fewer hardware resources because what we develop is faster, more compressed, or has a better architecture? Will we be able to make more money since we can take orders faster, process them, and ship them quicker? Will we save money by creating software that needs fewer people to maintain it, or roll out an infrastructure change that lowers the number of help desk calls?

If our software projects are for an industry-specific systems integrator, will the way we sequence tasks or level resources increase the profit margin to the company or buy us customer goodwill with a reputation for reliability? Will our project prowess ensure that we complete more projects faster and, thus, move us to a category with our suppliers in which we get a larger discount for hardware?

Motivating teams and making difficult decisions on the spot become easier when we understand specifically how the completion of this project is intended to benefit the company. When making the decision to fund this particular project over all of those that were in contention, why was this one more important than those that were tabled for later?

Usually the project manager is not given the answer to these critical questions, so you must learn to ask. The answer can alert you to whether time, money, or quality is the key driver on the project. When you know the answer, you can prepare workarounds, alternate solutions, and know where to spend your contingency reserves to keep your project aligned with the business reason for which it was created.

Don't Skip Vacations for the Project

Joe Zenevitch
New York, New York, U.S.

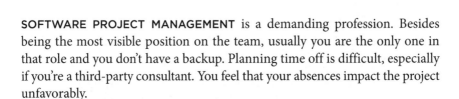

SOFTWARE PROJECT MANAGEMENT is a demanding profession. Besides being the most visible position on the team, usually you are the only one in that role and you don't have a backup. Planning time off is difficult, especially if you're a third-party consultant. You feel that your absences impact the project unfavorably.

To minimize this risk, novice project managers cancel their vacations, or in the worst cases, do not plan vacations at all. I've learned over time that you really need to take periodic vacations to get a break from the stressful conditions that are inherent in most projects. Over the course of your career, how bitterly do you resent the vacations you missed? But how foggy is your memory of the specific issues you sidestepped by remaining on the job?

I'm not suggesting that you should plan your next vacation with no regard for your project or project schedule. If it's only a three-week-duration project, you can wait. Taking a vacation the week before a major release would definitely be irresponsible. But, if your 9- to 12-month project tanks because you take a week or two off in the middle, then you are probably not managing it well in the first place.

Obviously, it is important to find and train someone to fill your role while you are away. He/she may not do things exactly as you would have done them, but your surrogate will be able to keep the project ship afloat and sailing in the right direction. You can make it known if you'd prefer to have major issues deferred until your return.

Your replacement could be a project manager from another team, but someone from your own team is probably the better choice. A team member will be more familiar with the project, and this gives him/her a tryout run serving in a leadership role. In some organizations, the business analyst can be a good fit as an interim "you." This person knows the requirements intimately, and should know the basic mechanics of how to run your development iterations if you've been involving the stakeholders at-large all along, as you should.

In agile development, the concept of the self-directed team is both important and powerful. The idea is that the project manager puts in place easy-to-understand and highly visible processes that the entire team follows. Over time, as the team adopts these processes, the project manager does less and less managing, and more and more facilitating. Essentially, removing obstacles and resolving issues replaces day-to-day micromanaging.

One of the delightful byproducts of a smoothly running, self-directed team is that the project manager's appropriately timed vacation can become almost a nonevent. Even if you are not around for a few days, the machine keeps running itself.

Certainly schedule your vacations to make sure you are available for project releases, but definitely take time off. And never cancel a vacation just because you think the project will grind to a halt without you.

Provide Regular
Time to Focus

James Leigh
Toronto, Ontario, Canada

SOFTWARE DEVELOPERS REGULARLY REPORT that interruptions such as meetings, demos, and urgent bug fixes keep them from completing their work. Typically, a person takes about 20 minutes to regain his train of thought after one of these interruptions. A 5-minute question actually costs 25 minutes, and a quick 10-minute meeting actually costs 30 minutes of potential work. Interruptions and recovery time consume 28% of a typical knowledge worker's day and can cause undue frustration and stress.

To help address this issue, set aside two hours a day (for example, between 10:00 a.m. and noon) that are interruption free. Alternately, you may be able to plan an entire day when no meetings, questions, email, phones, and other distractions are permitted, to allow developers to concentrate and focus on their work. Intel and IBM set aside Fridays, calling them "zero-email Fridays" and "Think Fridays," respectively.

It is equally important that developers know what their top two priorities are so they can plan their work for this period effectively. Even the best-intentioned developers could only randomly guess at what these are if they're not explicitly told what will bring real business value to the project.

Infomania (a debilitating state of information overload) is widely recognized as a major opponent to a developer's productivity. Programming requires that developers keep many things in their heads at once—everything from variables, class structures, APIs (application programming interfaces), utility methods, and even directory hierarchies. When a developer is interrupted, much of this information is "swapped out," and it requires considerable mental energy to regain it. This has a huge impact on productivity, and studies find that employees are not creating new ideas to the extent they used to because of infomania.

In addition, different types of distractions have varying degrees of impact on the developer's train of thought. One might be able to get up, use the restroom, get a cup of coffee and a sandwich, or even move to a whiteboard, while keeping all of the program data still actively circulating in the brain. In fact, the movement might help him/her see a new avenue to solve a problem.

Planned meetings are especially problematic for programmers, as they might waste time when they know there is an upcoming item on their schedule. They think, "why get started only to be interrupted in 30 minutes?" And great ideas that come during meetings may be lost, or stale, by the time the developer gets back to his computer to capture them.

Developers' productivity can also degrade by over 50% for each additional simultaneous project. Developers working on three or more projects often spend more time attending meetings to explain why they are not making any progress than getting any actual work done. When developers must contribute to multiple projects, make sure that they are guaranteed at least two full days on each project before switching to another. This will minimize the amount of time they must spend reintroducing themselves to each project.

Project Management Is Problem Management

Lorin Unger
Hoboken, New Jersey, U.S.

IN THE BEST OF CIRCUMSTANCES, software project management is a challenging and complex endeavor. Yet, I often see PMs make it even more difficult by having the wrong set of expectations for the role.

Plain and simple, project management is problem management. Were that not the case, there would be no need for project managers. Rather, a request for execution would be made and all the pieces (resources, technology, requirements, timeline, etc.) would simply align and the work would proceed smoothly to completion without any need for shepherding.

The truth is, our role exists because that is not the reality. Resources are overallocated, technologies and skill sets are incompatible, requirements are unclear, and timelines are unrealistic. I frequently work with PMs who view those types of issues as inconveniences, annoyances, or "problems" caused by external forces that are interfering with their work. If only *they* had done this, if only *they* had thought that out better, if only *they* would give me more time, then all these needless complications would be gone and I could finally get on with the business of project management.

Needless to say, these folks spend a lot of their time frustrated, tense, and irritable.

The fact of the matter is, smoothing all those needless bumps and complications is the business of project management. Our role is to plan better, think more clearly, and have a greater strategic vision that those who sponsor a project, and also those who work to deliver it. We're here because executing a project is an inherently messy business and individuals with our unique skills and temperaments are necessary to ensure that the inevitable difficulties get squashed, circumvented, or massaged into nonissues.

To complicate things further, this does not apply only to the mechanics of managing a project. Sometimes *people* need to be "massaged into nonissues" as well. The most challenging aspect of a project isn't necessarily the technology or timeline, but can be the personalities involved in the effort. This can be anyone from resources assigned to the project to a senior oversight committee.

Some easy archetypes: the "resentful resource," who seems perversely committed to undermining the PM's authority; the "nervous stakeholder," ever anxious, is impossible to soothe; or the "back-seat PM," a stakeholder or project participant who feels compelled to assert his/her opinion on how the project should be run at every possible opportunity.

It is, of course, beyond the scope of this tip to discuss how best to manage the various interpersonal issues that can arise in a project. Suffice it to say that the need to manage issues in this realm appears frequently, and is as much within the scope of our project management responsibilities as is understanding the work breakdown structure or maintaining an accurate project plan.

If we view these situations not as obstacles to doing the job but, more appropriately, as the heart of the job itself, the work will be smoother, calmer, and more tranquil. Relatively speaking, of course.

Empowering Developers: A Man Named Tim

Ken Sipe
St. Charles, Missouri, U.S.

OFTEN THE BEST THING a software project manager can do is set the vision, set the priorities, and get out of the way. Here's a true story about a man named Tim.

We found we needed another team member on our project, so we posted the opening and began to interview. One individual soon rose to the top of our candidate list.

His name was Tim. Tim stood out significantly from the other applicants, and it would have been a "no-brainer" decision to hire him. But, there was one dissenting vote. All resources hired into our department may rotate between any one of three project managers. One of those PMs had previous experience working with Tim and indicated that he lacked motivation. She painted a picture of Tim web surfing regularly while on the job, and being a slacker.

This was a tough situation. When making a hiring decision, more weight would normally be applied to a project manager's personal experience with the candidate as compared to a cold interview. However, from a technical perspective, Tim's skills significantly exceeded those of other candidates. He was hired despite the dissenting vote. The project was run using an agile development methodology, so we had an open meeting at the start of the iteration.*

The opening meeting has several main purposes:

1. Stories† are created and their priority is established and communicated, based on user input.

---

* *Iteration*: A short period of time chosen by an agile project team (a week, two weeks, a month, etc.) during which a key requirement chosen by the customer will be developed, tested, and then delivered to the customer for approval or comment. The next iteration will then begin to develop the next most important requirement and/or correct the work done in the preceding iteration.

† *Story*: A high-level description of a software requirement, usually broken down into single developer tasks, with just enough information to allow a developer to estimate how long it will take to create, test, and/or implement it.

2. A team vision of the project scope is created through the stories, and good acceptance criteria are established.

3. Stories are broken down into tasks and estimated by the developer who is to complete the task.

After the meeting, the tasks are entered into the task tracking system. The significance of the task tracking system is often misunderstood. It is used for developers to see what tasks are started. If they have finished their own tasks early, they move on by "stealing" (or completing) a task not yet begun by the originally assigned developer.

Tim turned out to be an outstanding hire. He out-produced everyone else on the team. The most obvious measure of his value was in the number of tasks he "stole" from other developers. Completing more tasks meant the project finished quicker.

So the question is, why would another PM see Tim as unproductive? On closer inspection, it became evident that the Tim-basher had a management style that was excessively controlling. She would "spoon-feed" tasks to developers and then leave the team workspace to attend meetings. Tim was so fast that he would complete his assigned task immediately. Without any further direction regarding project priorities or tasks he could begin next, he was left idle.

You'll be amazed what a good team can do with a clear vision, well-defined acceptance criteria, and shared project priorities not determined by a lone software project manager but known, documented, and managed by the entire team. Sometimes the best thing for the PM to do is get out of the way. Do you manage a Tim?

Clever Code Is
Hard to Maintain

David Wood
Fredericksburg, Virginia, U.S.

DEVELOPERS ARE OFTEN ASKED TO CREATE MIRACLES. They must find clever ways to make today's project code work with yesterday's antiquated legacy software containing multiple patches. And through skill and ingenuity, they may create numerous lines of clever code that finally get the job done. But clever code may only create future maintenance problems due to the code's length and complexity. There may be a better way.

If you are a project manager new to software development, don't be afraid to let developers explore new languages and development tools. Allow them this freedom, because this is how they discover innovative ways to improve their coding practices and results. They may be able to design a software solution to your legacy interface problem that is faster and has fewer lines of code to test and maintain. This is certainly an advantage to your project.

There are innovative new programming languages that can perform the same functions as your current ones with substantially fewer lines of code. This is valuable in that a simpler code structure is easier to test, can be self-defining, is smaller to store, and is easier to maintain.

Obviously, there are some concerns about adding new languages and platforms within your organization. Will this new code truly solve the problem for the current software or upgrade under development? Will it interface long-term with the existing software used in your legacy databases, user interfaces within the organization, and third-party software in which the company has already invested?

Are there other developers on the team or the department who will be able to create software in this language or on this platform? Is there adequate product support from language authors? Will there be timely updates and improvements?

Even if you are not familiar with programming yourself, don't be reluctant to allow programmers to embrace new languages. If the new language can trace its tortured lineages back to C or Java (or any other common way of doing things), it is probably going to be relatively painless to merge it into your current practices.

However, be sure to document any new practices within your code. Otherwise, your code base and the documentation about the code may diverge to the point that the best way to understand the system is to look at the code itself. This is called a "loss of coupling" between the software components and system metadata. And when there is inadequate documentation to maintain your software system, it must be replaced.

Encourage your project team developers to be innovative, but not clever to the point of excessive complexity. Being too clever makes it hard on those who follow. If later developers can't read the code, how can they be expected to maintain it? Any given programmer may try to be clever to enhance his job security, but no project manager will benefit from it.

Code that is too clever will ultimately be too hard to maintain. That leads to maintenance failure and a costly reworking of your software systems.

Managing Human Factors in IT Project Management

James Graham, PMP
Ta' l-Ibrag, Malta

AS SOFTWARE PROJECT MANAGERS, we obsess over the schedule details. We huddle with our teammates to try to anticipate risk factors that could derail our projects. We crunch numbers to see if we can squeeze the project deliverables out of the allocated budget. But we tend to overlook, or ignore, the most prevalent cause of project failure: the human factor.

From errors, to accidents, to out-and-out nonperformance, human failure to perform can often be tied to our tendency to repeat our past behaviors. If it worked successfully for us last time, it should work again. There is an old saying: "For he who is a hammer, every problem is a nail." Psychological research shows that people under the influence of stress may revert to the learning or experiences that are hammer-like, because they found success with them in the past. What is more stressful than undertaking a new software project?

Because the objective of most projects is to create a new product, service, or solution, agility and flexibility of mind and working style are major positive behaviors to encourage instead of repeating past actions. Following old processes may be counterproductive when you're faced with a new, different challenge.

Consider a business analyst who is highly experienced in one formal software project management methodology. Intellectually, he may agree with his developers' explanation of why a more agile approach to software development makes sense. But when faced with time pressures that appear to compromise the project, he may revert to using some favorite techniques that worked well in past, non-software-related experiences.

Bank supervisors report that reversing numbers is a common error, especially when employees are not 100% focused due to work-related or personal stress. Knowing this human tendency, the wise project manager will carefully check estimates, budgets, and other documents for these types of careless, but human, errors.

What leads to stress on your project team? It could be personal, such as having an argument with a spouse before leaving for work, or financial pressures at home. Perhaps there are family worries about health or children.

Work-related encounters can also be stress inducing. It could be something as minor as being late to a key stakeholder meeting and forgetting to bring an important document. Or, it could be concerns from job security to worries that the coding and testing for this project cannot be completed on target.

Stress leads to past behavior, not active problem-solving actions. As the software project manager, it is your job to be on the lookout for symptoms of stress that can lead your team members to regress to old behaviors. By having active conversations with them and carefully managing their work environment, you can prevent or help minimize the effects of stress.

People are human, so human emotions are natural in the workplace. But only people can develop software. So, nurture and manage your human capital as carefully as you monitor and protect your nonhuman resources.

Use a Wiki

Adrian Wible
New York, New York, U.S.

WIKIS ARE A GREAT MECHANISM to centralize access to your project information. Hopefully, the wiki will be updated multiple times daily and will always be open in a window on team members' desktops.

To prevent you from wasting any precious brain cells that may be needed for the actual project work, I've provided some suggestions for pages you might include on your wiki. While creating these, you are sure to have ideas about customizing the site for your own software project:

- **Stakeholders.** Have space for topics such as up-to-the-minute project status, short-term issues, long-term issues, risk, budget tracking, and milestone achievements.

- **Developers.** Add information such as the connection string to connect to the QA database. Fellow programmers won't wasting time trying to locate the code from other random sources. Team members can share information on topics like coding standards, build and deployment procedures, common pitfalls, and use of advanced coding techniques such as dependency injection.

- **General information.** The software project manager should add the help desk phone number, team roles and responsibilities, and individual team member contact information here.

- **Team calendars.** Use this site to post team calendars. One great trick is to use an embedded iFrame pointing to a Google calendar.

- **Meeting minutes.** Archive meeting minutes so the team can easily refresh its memory on the details covered in past meetings. Also, team members can quickly reference the minutes to research or prepare for future meetings.

- **Meeting agenda.** Set up a process for stakeholders to suggest future agenda items online. Subject, of course, to the approval of the software project manager, the necessity for the item to be presented to the entire team, and the time limitations of the next meeting.

- **Business analyst.** Often this person is not colocated in the developer work-space. This is a perfect space to centralize access to working documents and domain artifacts that can be accessed from multiple locations.

- **Testers.** The organizational structure may separate testing responsibility from the programmer. This site can provide a clearinghouse between the two teams. Post topics like how to use testing tools such as Selenium, QTP, and Quality Center. Bug-tracking procedures can be developed and discussed online, and the final decisions posted here.

Some tips:

- Don't duplicate information. If the information lies elsewhere, link to that information instead of copying it into the wiki.

- Keep an eye on the volume of changes to make sure the information is not getting stale. If it does, people will stop using the wiki.

- Try to make your information real-time-data–driven if possible. Look for project management tools that include a wiki interface to enable creation of charts and status that is driven from the actual project data. This gives real-time status for the work in progress.

Any time you send project information via email, particularly with file attachments (documents, project plans, budget information, etc.), you should consider whether the team wiki would be a more appropriate place to exchange and archive that information.

The Missing Link

Paul Waggoner, MBA, PMP, MCSE, CHP, CHSS
Waukee, Iowa, U.S.

SOFTWARE PROJECT MANAGERS AGREE that one of their most difficult challenges is keeping team members properly engaged in the details of the project, and on top of their assigned tasks and schedules. They understand that team members are conflicted between the routine, operational responsibilities of processing daily work, troubleshooting problems, coordinating departmental issues, and answering everyday communications, versus completing the time-sensitive work of project development.

Although being selected for a project team may initially be seen as a compliment, many developers feel that participation on a team is a major distraction from day-to-day duties. When push comes to shove, a developer may openly admit that daily maintenance and support of assigned systems are more important to him/her than performing project task work.

As a project manager, your first impulse is to conclude that this person does not belong on the team if your work can't, or won't, be given a clear priority. However, most organizations have limited numbers of subject matter experts (SMEs), so changing team members or locating a more dedicated one may not be an option.

Here are a few simple suggestions to help with this problem:

- Make sure all management levels support the goals and objectives of the project.

- Modify the subject matter expert job description to include "perform as team member on various projects as needed," instead of "perform other duties as assigned."

- Have management and Human Resources emphasize this change, and make sure all supervisors weigh project activity achievements heavily in future performance evaluations.

- At the beginning of each new project, the software project manager, the departmental manager or supervisor, the sponsor, or another key stakeholder should send out a personalized communiqué inviting each team member to participate in the project. This letter or email should explain the high-level objectives of the project being undertaken, and the high-level responsibilities of this specific team member.

- Announce that at the successful conclusion of this project, each team member will receive a Certificate of Recognition and Achievement suitable for framing. Note that a second copy will be placed in his/her Human Resources file to be referenced during quarterly performance reviews.

- The departmental manager's boss should make it clear that projects advance organizational goals at an even more important level than the routine information technology tasks do.

- The executive should specifically request that the departmental manager help the project team member free up time on a regular basis to complete the project activities, even if his regular tasks must be temporarily off-loaded to another member of the IT group.

It should be clearly understood that those who successfully participate in projects are "going the extra mile" for the organization and should be recognized and rewarded. Those who participate successfully in large or small projects should be singled out for praise. As they say in the agile world, this puts the "art of the possible" in proper perspective, aligning organizational objectives with employee motivations.

Estimate, Estimate, Estimate

Richard Sheridan
Ann Arbor, Michigan, U.S.

SO OFTEN IN PROJECT MANAGEMENT, we get an estimate for a project at the beginning of the project (when we know the least) and then never revisit that estimate during the course of the project (when we know more than we did at the beginning). Worse, we never compare our original estimate with actual results to hone our future skills.

In our practice at my organization, we estimate once a week on every project. Even for those tasks we have previously estimated but haven't worked on yet, we estimate again. Why do we do this? There are several reasons:

- We get better at estimating the more we do it.

- Sometimes we now know more and that helps our estimating.

- Sometimes we learn we didn't know as much as we thought we did, and that helps our estimating.

- Often when a new technology is involved, early estimates have "fear" built in; as we learn more about the new technology, the fear-based component lessens.

- Estimating is a great "conversation" in our world, since we estimate as a group activity.

Finally, the best way to get better at estimating is to make sure you also keep track of actuals so that the team gets feedback on how well it did in estimating. My only warning: you can't use this information to punish the team! True accountability around estimating doesn't involve getting people to hit their estimate, but rather to have them warn you as soon as they think they are going to miss.

Here is a simple game you can play to drive home the power of estimating and feedback. Get three different empty jars of increasing size and fill them with jelly beans. Record how many jelly beans it takes to fill up every jar.

Get together a group you are trying teach about estimating and ask members to estimate the number of jelly beans in the smallest jar. When I teach this, I have people work in pairs.

Give them only a short time to come up with an estimate and then have them *write it down*. Collect the data by having each pair read its estimates aloud. Write the estimates down on a whiteboard or flipchart. Do the same for the second and third jars of jelly beans.

Finally, tell the group members that this is a good way to do estimating, thank them for their input, and ask if there are any questions before you move on. It never fails. Someone will ask how many jelly beans there actually are in each jar. *They want to know*! Let them dangle a while and then tell them how silly they are. After all, it's just a jar of jelly beans.

Now you have them right where you want them. Ask them how many times they've had the data to give feedback to their team on *far more important* topics and they scoffed and dismissed it as unimportant. Overlooking feedback to their teams will not happen again.

Developers Unite—PMOs Are Advancing

Angelo Valle
Rio de Janeiro, Brazil

IF YOU'RE A SOFTWARE DEVELOPER, you are probably convinced that a more responsive, adaptable framework is your best chance of producing working software. Unfortunately, the rest of the world is moving to have a more standardized approach throughout all departments. This is good news for everyone except software developers.

A recently emerging concept in organizational structure is the project management office (PMO). This global phenomenon tasks a small group of individuals with the supervision and support of enterprise projects and programs. The group's purpose is to introduce consistency in documents and templates, standardize reporting processes, and provide a uniform way to add business value through projects.

PMOs are intended to be centers of intelligence and coordination. They link strategic business objectives to employees' actions within departmental projects through unified portfolio management, program management, and project management practices. This is a good thing for your job security.

The PMO's functions within the business can be:

- **Strategic.** In this role, the members of the Project Management Office complete functions of identification, selection, and prioritization of the projects that are most closely aligned with the organization's strategic planning.

- **Directive.** To fulfill their directive responsibilities, PMO employees define guidelines, standards, and templates. They evaluate and choose how software project managers should apply the best practices, tools, techniques, and software to successfully complete the goals of their development teams.

- **Supportive.** The PMO provides support to team members and project managers. This may manifest itself as training classes, adjusting templates and documents to make them work in all departments, or working with a project manager on staffing or other human resource issues.

Project Management Offices are not identical from corporation to corporation around the world. Each business is at a different developmental stage with its project management practices. So, the common name of PMO may encompass numerous hybrid responsibilities drawn from the aforementioned list, or unique ones not mentioned.

The PMO provides guidance in suitable standardized and validated tools, techniques, and software, thereby reducing problems due to uncertainty and the growing emphasis on cheaper/better/faster projects. The PMO applies a standardized methodology where necessary and effective: project identification, data collection, analysis, information gathering, distribution, reporting, risk management, procurement, quality, and other project management knowledge areas such as documentation and communications.

The theme of economic success through a PMO model is a hot topic in international congresses, seminars, and recently published papers. Academic discussions are prolific, because of a growing need to match university experiences with actual "real world" practices. The students of today are the developers of tomorrow.

PMOs are here to stay. If you are currently a software developer, you should be proactive in opening a dialog with your PMO. Communicate your professional success stories and the uniqueness of the software development process. If you don't, you are liable to be saddled with methods, documentation requirements, and procedures that don't fit your needs. Fast, good, high-quality software is in everyone's best interest.

Value Results,
Not Just Effort

Venkat Subramaniam
Broomfield, Colorado, U.S.

DEVELOPING SOFTWARE TAKES A LOT OF EFFORT. However, if you hear someone brag, "I work on an application with over 3 million lines of code," ask him or her how many of those lines of code are really needed.

Often, extra code is added with some perceived extensibility* in mind. Extensibility is important, but if not done correctly, it can have the opposite effect. It can delay your current project.

Extra, out-of-scope code is a symptom of software project managers who reward only extra time and extra effort. If you routinely insist that the programmers work long hours, be sure they are actually producing additional, useable results.

I like my lawn to be green, and rely on my sprinkler system to water it every day. My first summer in Colorado, I noticed that one of my maple trees had lost most of its leaves. Assuming that the hot and arid conditions were the reason, I watered longer but noticed no improvement. The expert I consulted asked me, "How frequently and how long do you water?" Hearing my answer, he said, "That's the problem! Reduce the duration and frequency by half, and you will see improvement."

I was killing the tree with excessive water. Having slightly less water actually helps these trees. It builds their resistance and helps their growth. Two weeks after following his advice, my tree was healthy and full of leaves.

Your programmers are like maple trees when it comes to work time. Give them small, but adequate amounts of time and fewer broadly defined tasks, and they flourish. Give them larger task chunks and ask them to routinely work extra

---

* *Extensibility*: A systems design principle where future growth is taken into consideration. The ability to create and implement additional features is maximized while coding the currently needed functionality.

hours, and they begin to wilt. Plus, they tend to overwrite and complicate the code, since they have too much time on their hands.

I worked for a manager who focused on how long people worked. Working a Saturday morning, or staying late in the evening, was more important to him than what employees were actually producing. It is impossible to be a productive and effective programmer for 12 hours or more a day.

In another group, the manager kept us to a traditional eight-hour work schedule. Yes, there were days we stayed late, but those were exceptions rather than the norm. Employees knew they were not required to work long hours but had to provide their committed deliverables on schedule. So, we were focused and less distracted, prioritized our work well, and used our time effectively. Even though developer capabilities were about the same in both groups, we got more accomplished in the second group than in the one where we worked to exhaustion.

Encourage programmers to report the progress they make, rather than how long they work. Let them know that you care about getting results rather than keeping track of how long they spent at the computer. Once your team members realize that you are a results-oriented manager and not a "put in hours" manager, their focus will shift to achieving results rather than merely clocking hours at work.

Software Failure Is Organizational Failure

Brian Sletten
Beverly Hills, California, U.S.

WE ALWAYS BLAME DEVELOPERS when things go wrong with software projects in an organization. When deadlines are missed, or when what is delivered has more bugs than an entomologist's wildest fantasy, it may seem that the team is not good enough, smart enough, productive enough, or up to the challenge. While individual teams may deserve a fair amount of criticism, you cannot forget that successful software projects require active and adequate participation by all stakeholders.

Everyone's participation is crucial, because in order to stave off failure, you need to know who is building what, when, and why. You need to add business functionality in deliberate, prioritized ways. You need to catch problems with poorly captured and expressed requirements. You need to nip latent impediments in the bud by spotting people who are potential blockers, noting communication failures, and soothing overwhelmed (but overeager) development teams.

Developing software requires valid metrics, clear communication, and engaged business and executive stakeholders. They must be involved in software delivery efforts and assume partial responsibility for both positive and negative outcomes. The software project manager needs to measure and track success and failure records. Teams that consistently deliver can be trusted to do so again. Teams that seldom deliver require more oversight, further training, and realignment, or perhaps some members must be shown the door.

However, allow software teams time to clean up their own messes. As they rush toward various releases,* they will incur what wiki pioneer Ward Cunningham calls "technical debt." Like real debt, if it is not paid down consistently and responsibly, it will become unwieldy and require too much attention to service.

---

* *Releases*: The agile development method of software development creates specific functionality within several short time frames. During each time period, requirements analysis, planning, design, coding, unit testing, and acceptance testing are performed. At the end of this time, a workable feature is "released," or shown to the customer.

Each iteration[†] of work should include new business functionality, as well as a sanctioned effort to refactor some of the hacks[‡] that inevitably show up in the code. This is neither a license to goof off, nor the sign of a bad team. It is simply a programming reality that must be routinely addressed with full support from the executive stakeholders.

The organization must commit to tracking industry trends, acquiring tools, and adopting practices that demonstrate productive influences on how programmers work. Encourage developers to expand their knowledge, both on and off the clock. Playing around with new tools, being trained, attending high-value conferences, and reading books and blogs are all necessary components of the constant effort required by this field.

Organizing team lunches where members share knowledge and promote new ideas is a great, inexpensive way to foster growth. Software engineers who feel supported by their employers tend to be more loyal and willing to go the extra mile. They are also more likely to be able and ready to respond to changes in requirements and technical landscapes.

The software industry has a lot of work to do to help its practitioners be more consistent in the delivery of high-quality, on-time releases. Organizations that build software must be engaged in the process at all levels to improve their own chances for continued, repeatable success.

---

† *Iteration*: A short period of time chosen by an agile project team (a week, two weeks, a month, etc.) during which a key requirement chosen by the customer will be developed, tested, and then delivered to the customer for approval or comment. The next iteration will then begin to develop the next most important requirement and/or correct the work done in the preceding iteration.

‡ *Refactoring a hack*: Going back to reprogram a quick, workable fix created to get a software feature working, but which needs further internal refinement to facilitate its long-term use and support.

A Voice from the Other Side

Marty Skomal, MPA
Omaha, Nebraska, U.S.

WHILE IT'S GREAT TO HEAR FROM DEVELOPERS and software project managers, you might find it equally advantageous to hear from the guy with the metaphorical purse. I'm the customer.

Software developers have now infiltrated the realm of nonprofit and government sectors, with promises of low-cost, web-based ways of doing business using fancy technologies that have heretofore have been too expensive, too elaborate, and beyond the comfort level of our employees and constituents.

Nonprofit and governmental agencies, subsisting on a shoestring and a few paper clips, can be seduced by these automated possibilities, but there is a trap. In an attempt to have it all, you can end up with nothing workable and longing for the days of a shoebox and a pack of 3×5 index cards to house your data.

For example, my agency decided to move from a paper-based grant application process to an online one. Forms would be submitted directly to the agency and downloaded into our database, avoiding manual data entry errors, lowering cost, and bypassing mailing inconveniences for constituents. We could also view applications online during their preparation process and provide assistance before submission.

Our software developers were eager to point out how they could automate additional aspects of the grant application process, such as vetting potential organizations against eligibility criteria before allowing them into the system, ensuring that deadlines were met, and forcing expenses and income to balance before allowing the Submit button to activate.

Our core needs were simply to import data, verify its accuracy, and communicate back via email that we had received their proposals. However, we were encouraged to program our system so that applications submitted after the deadline would be rejected. By building in rigid requirements, we lost the flexibility to be responsive and service oriented. Plus, once the system blocked an application after the deadline passed, we were totally unable to import it into our database without contacting the developers to perform a special override.

We should have started with a simpler system and added levels of complexity as we became familiar with its capabilities. Instead, we ended up with part of a nonfunctional spaceship when all we needed was a complete bicycle.

We walked away from that system and now use a vendor with a more stable system that has fewer features. We adjusted our internal procedures to fit the system rather than building software from scratch to keep our old procedures intact. We now see our online grants system as a way to receive data and manipulate it in our own database, rather than as a monument to all that is technically possible but not necessarily useful.

To avoid leading your not-for-profit clients astray:

- Allow them to plan, build slowly, and test, test, test.

- Resist the temptation to advise them to over-automate simple tasks.

- Be the development team who cares about understanding your user's needs.

Please try to understand what your not-for-profit client can successfully implement, before exhausting your entire technology toolbag on an emerging market.

Keep Your Perspective

James Graham, PMP
Ta' l-Ibrag, Malta

WHEN GATHERING BUSINESS REQUIREMENTS FROM USERS, it is common to hear "the system is slow," "the application is unreliable and crashes," "it does everything we don't need and nothing we do need," "the menu structure is cumbersome," and "it takes too many keystrokes to do a simple task."

Most software project managers empathize with users. We try to make them feel better by suggesting solutions that will appear to remove their pain. I believe that this approach, while well intended, is intrinsically wrong. Further, it reduces the probability of a successful outcome in the subsequent project.

Some people say that the point of gathering business requirements is to provide a custom-designed solution, which in turn reduces end-user frustration. I would agree that this is a worthy goal. However, a fatal flaw occurs if the project manager who decides the best solution bases his decision on a heartfelt desire to make the users feel better. In reality, project managers may not have trained themselves to keep an unbiased perspective.

Perspective means looking for the best solution, not the fix that feels right to the users. Remember, users have a deep understanding of their business area and can make impressive contributions to a project by sharing that knowledge. But how should we use their input?

When I worked as a management consultant in London, my experienced colleagues used to mentor me on the importance of objectivity. Their wisdom was based on the truism that most experts like to show how clever they are, when often they should spend more time using their skills to ask the right questions to uncover the root problem. If you don't unmask the real problem, your attempts to remove it will only swat at the symptoms.

We all are at risk to succumb to this mistake. Recently, I was asked to design a management development program for a large organization. My immediate impulse was to rush to address its pain points speedily, by suggesting that we look at an existing program I own. I knew I could easily adapt it to cure the issues that were creating so much irritation for my client.

Fortunately, my self-restraint kicked in. I spent an hour talking to the senior managers about their real challenges. After I stepped back to listen to the business problem, not merely the end-user complaints that indicated something was amiss, I recommended an entirely different solution. It was more suited to their needs and addressed their core issues.

The next time you are confronted by frustrated users, take a deep breath. Allow them to vent their dissatisfaction with the surface symptoms they encounter day-to-day. These irritations are real. Then ask them a series of questions to get to the underlying, root causes of their frustration. Avoid the temptation to make them feel better by providing a quick fix. It is in their best interests for you to make sure you are aiming for the right target before you plan your project solution trajectory.

How Do You Define "Finished"?

Brian Sam-Bodden
Scottsdale, Arizona, U.S.

IT IS HARD FOR A SOFTWARE DEVELOPMENT TEAM TO SUCCEED if there isn't a clear definition of what success means. For developers, success entails delivering a product that meets customer expectations. However, to define total project success, we need an accurate, shared definition among the larger project team of what it means to "finish the project."

To embrace the overall project scope, the core tenet of traditional, iterative software development is "divide and conquer." The project is broken into deliverables, which are then divided into work packages. Those are ultimately broken into activities assigned to a specific person.

Using an agile approach with one- to several-week iterations, or work periods, the necessity to consider overall project scope can be masked. Finishing the goals of one iteration can be clearly set out as creating working software that passes unit tests, possibly clears limited integration tests, and allows promised software features to be demo'd to the stakeholders for their approval and feedback.

The problem is that at the macro level, a project has many other considerations beyond the code and its accompanying tests. Using the traditional waterfall method, testing was relegated to the end of a project and became a flaw in the process. In a more agile approach, developers may erroneously defer or dismiss all the nonprogramming items or activities as not having a place in their view of what a software project entails.

Some of these items may be unit and integration testing between a newly created component/feature and the components/features created in prior iterations.

These often-overlooked integrations underscore a fundamental problem for development teams. The complexity of software seems to be geometrically proportional to the number of component interconnections. Don't ignore the time needed to craft a demo environment, and do write user-level/acceptance testing scripts and create accompanying documentation. No matter how light your methodology, shippable software requires a certain level of documentation.

When these items are not ignored, the macro definition of what it means to be "finished" differs significantly from the accumulated finishing of a set of features within an iteration. And, the delta created from a buildup of those missing items per iteration can alter the way a feature is implemented, tested, and perceived by the customer.

Let's not overburden our developers with administrative or business issues. The underlying concept we need to spread is that iterations are not just for software developers. They must be coordinated with tasks important to the larger, general software project team members. Business analysts, software project managers, and quality testers must coordinate their crucial activities with those of the developers.

The person responsible for this coordination is the software project manager, who must understand and spread the overall definition of what it means to be finished at the macro level so that the non-code-based activities are performed side by side with the weekly iteration work. The project manager must be the arbiter between the development team and the other stakeholders to define what it truly means to be "finished."

The 60/60 Rule

David Wood
Fredericksburg, Virginia, U.S.

WE OFTEN PRETEND that software development is the most important part of the software life cycle. Methodologies abound for development. Books, magazine articles, and blogs focus on development. Development, however, is just not where the money is.

Fully 60% of the life cycle costs of software systems come from maintenance, with a relatively measly 40% coming from development. That is an average, of course. The actual cost of maintenance may vary from 40% to 80%, depending on the system type and the environment it is deployed into. During maintenance, 60% of the costs on average relate to user-generated enhancements (changing requirements), 23% to migration activities, and 17% to bug fixes.

The 60% of life cycle costs related to maintenance, coupled with the fact that 60% of maintenance activities relate to enhancements, gives us the so-called 60/60 Rule, one of the few proposed "laws" of software maintenance.

Migration activities include moving systems to new hardware or software environments. Migration is, of course, a type of changing requirement. Factoring that into our estimates points out an interesting fact: over 80% of maintenance activities relate in some way to changing requirements.

Naturally, the ability to change code suggests that one should understand it first. Understanding changes to be made is a major activity during maintenance. Roughly 30% of total maintenance time is spent on understanding an existing software product. The development of understanding applies to all forms of maintenance: changing requirements, migration, and bug fixes.

Understanding is a cost we must pay to maintain code that someone else wrote, or we wrote long enough ago that we no longer have an intimate knowledge of it. During maintenance, understanding code takes the place of new design work found during development for most tasks.

The 60/60 Rule should prompt us to rethink the focus of software development, as well as maintenance. The tendency to address development activities may not yield the most impressive gains. Boehm's early assertion in the early 1980s that proper software engineering discipline can reduce defects by up to 75% may be true (although I seriously doubt it), and became the basis for much work toward development methodologies, but so what?

A good methodology may reduce bugs (17% of the total maintenance effort), but not address migration, enhancement time, or cost at all. To reduce maintenance costs, we have to address the costs associated with understanding code, adjusting code to new requirements, and/or migrating code to new environments.

The 60/60 Rule suggests that we should focus our efforts on creating systems that are maintainable. Our software must be designed to change so systems become flexible in the face of new requirements. Designing such systems is one of the next great challenges in software engineering.

We know at least part of the answer. The software components need to become less tightly coupled with one another, much the way the components of the World Wide Web are bound together at the last possible moment and in a flexible manner.

We Have Met the Enemy... and He Is Us

Barbee Davis, MA, PHR, PMP
Omaha, Nebraska, U.S.

CARTOONIST WALT KELLEY, who inked the long-running comic strip *Pogo*, is famous for the quote, "We have met the enemy...and he is us." Nowhere is this sentiment more accurate than when describing a software project manager who is new to the software development process. Here's how to avoid having "the enemy" be you:

- As a project manager, you expect your team members to estimate the amount of time it will take them to complete a specific task. It is detrimental to the schedule if they go too far over the budgeted time. One of your tasks on the project is to hold meetings to drive team communication. You need to demonstrate the ability to estimate and deliver the meetings as meticulously as you expect your developers to estimate and deliver their code.

  When your meetings run long, you are stealing the precious programming time developers count on to meet your project schedule deadlines.

- If your project team spoke a foreign language, you would take some lessons and get a translator. Your developers do not speak your language. Buy a book, take a class, make Google your friend, and find a developer who has the gift to explain complex things in a simple way. You cannot bluff your way through this project without learning some of the concepts, terms, and challenges your team faces.

- Regardless of the perfect methodology you used to build toasters and cars, develop pharmaceuticals, or even construct skyscrapers, it won't work here. Let the trusted members of your team explain about agile methodologies. They aren't new or risky. But they are your best chance at having a working product at the end of your project.

- Developers are craftsmen and artists. They work differently than accountants, attorneys, or bank tellers. When they are meeting in pairs and talking animatedly, they are actually working. When they are bouncing a ball against a wall or doodling on a whiteboard, they may be crafting a solution to an architecture problem that can't be solved by staring at a computer screen. Give them space.

- Your team will work odd hours. We've all seen the cashier at the local food emporium switch with her replacement: she opens the register and exchanges the money drawer, and the new cashier is up and running. A programmer can't switch places with a cohort and just pick up where his teammate left off. When your team member is feverishly at work, leave him or her alone. Researchers say it may take an hour or more for the person to regain productivity if interrupted.

- It is unnecessary to have every person program in exactly the same programming language. Some endeavors are better approached with newer languages that require fewer lines of code to write, test, store on your servers, and maintain. Don't refuse to let your developers use the best tool for the job.

Open your mind to this new world of software development, and you can be a support for your software development team, not the enemy.

Work in Cycles

James Leigh
Toronto, Ontario, Canada

OUR BODIES ARE FULL OF NATURAL CYCLES, and our productivity is no different. The human brain cannot focus on any single issue for more than a few hours at a time. Ideal workdays are designed to ensure that the body has time to rest and refocus every 90 to 180 minutes. Productivity has been shown to degrade after about 90–120 minutes of work, requiring the brain to change focus before productivity can increase.

The most effective software projects are created in environments that ensure that developers are mentally productive. However, many things that contribute to developers' productivity are out of the control of their software project manager. You can't ensure that they eat appropriately, or sleep enough hours at night. However, a project manager can help ensure that a developer's productivity does not degrade during the day, by encouraging frequent breaks and providing opportunity for nutrition. The old saying that developers are driven by their stomachs is true.

Studies also show that projects are more successful when broken into iterations. By creating weekly or monthly subprojects—complete with goals, priorities, feedback, and releases—software bugs can be mitigated and developer satisfaction can be increased. Breaking the work into smaller iterations provides opportunities to track progress and acknowledge good results. It also gives everyone on the team the opportunity to reflect, give feedback to one another, and improve communication.

Every cycle should include a planning stage, an action stage, a completion stage, and a reward stage. Before beginning on any action item, ask yourself or your team these questions: why, when, how, what, and who? Why are we doing this? When is this going to be complete? How are we going to do this? What are we going to accomplish? Who on our team will be responsible for each portion of the item? With proper communication and understanding, the action stage can be effective and productive, contributing to the overall success of the project.

Once a task or action item is complete, get outside feedback. If one or two members of the team completed the work, get another team member to review it (peer review). If the entire team completed the work, get feedback from other stakeholders (preferably end-users). The final stage of any cycle is the reward stage; this is important for the sustainable health of any team or individual. As a battery must be recharged after use, the brain and body must be rewarded through recognition or acknowledgment of work.

As a software project manager, you must guide the team through project cycles, ensuring that every person understands the plan and gets the feedback he or she needs. Furthermore, each individual must follow his or her own daily cycle of planning, doing, completing, and being rewarded. The manager must ensure that all team members get the attention, information, and time they need to keep their productivity at its best. This way, you can ensure that your team is functioning at its full capacity.

To Thine Own Self Be True

Harry Tucker
Matawan, New Jersey, U.S.

ANY OF US WHO HAVE TRAVELED ON COMMERCIAL AIRCRAFT remember that during the safety demonstration we are told to put our oxygen masks on first, and then to assist an elderly person or child with his or her mask. If we struggle to put the other person's mask on before ours, we may succumb to oxygen deprivation before succeeding, and we all die. By putting ours on quickly, we are empowered to put 100% effort into taking care of others, and everyone lives.

I have witnessed many wonderful projects collapse over the years, even though the perfect storm of success was at the feet of those involved. The projects in question had:

- Unlimited market potential

- A superior product

- An empowered team enabled with phenomenal capability

However, the project manager had lost control of him-/herself and, therefore, could not take care of the team. The opportunity died of oxygen deprivation, so to speak, and the project failed.

To manage or lead teams (and there are sharp differences), software project managers need to be in complete control of themselves. They must have a strong understanding of their own personal purpose, vision, and mission, as well as personal and professional goals. When a solid personal life structure is in place, the manager's life is empowered. Without such empowerment, the manager is easily swept away by the challenges of living (both inside and outside the office). Then, an otherwise intelligent, talented manager loses focus on the management tasks at hand.

When that happens, various symptoms start to appear, one cascading upon the next:

1. The manager becomes visibly distracted and starts to feel out of control.

2. Not feeling in control, he/she doesn't feel empowered to stand up and do what is needed to protect the project.

3. The unprotected team starts to experience communication breakdowns.

4. Communication breakdowns lead to slipped (not aligned with the original project baseline) tasks.

5. Slipped tasks, and a manager unable to bring things back under control, lead to team despair.

6. Team morale fails, adding further complexity to a project that is already out of control.

I personally take time on a daily, weekly, and semi-annual basis to review where I am in my life. My daily and weekly reviews help me keep on track as far as short-term goals are concerned. My semi-annual retreat (white space planning, as some people call it) provides me with an opportunity to assess my long-term goals, personally and professionally, to make sure I am still on track.

While life will always throw curveballs at all of us, having short- and long-term goals helps provide us with targets that help us realign our personal and professional course after the turbulence has passed. With such a plan in hand, we are enabled to focus more on the tasks at hand, including managing our teams, to empower them toward success.

The oxygen masks have fallen—who are you helping first?

Meetings Don't Write Code

William J. Mills
Castro Valley, California, U.S.

TOO OFTEN, people who could be doing something more productive are trapped in meetings—meetings that have wandered off their intended purpose, run over time, or trapped an entire team in the room when a more limited set of people would be just as effective. Only schedule meetings that have a specific purpose, and only include people on the invitation list who need to be there. Here's an obvious list of things to avoid, as software project manager, when you are planning your team meetings:

- **Chit-chat.** If you have participants who use this time to have informal project-related exchanges, remind them to come a few minutes early or plan to spend time together after the meeting. You can't afford for the entire group to wait until they finish chatting.

- **Not getting in, getting done, and getting out.** Plan a clear agenda that is distributed beforehand. If you assemble the entire team, be sure your topics are relevant to everyone.

- **Diving too deep.** It is good to bring up risk issues or roadblocks that have arisen. However, this is not the place to hammer out the solutions. Form smaller groups, or designate the appropriate team member, to pursue the issue after the meeting.

  The minute software engineers start talking about specific implementation details, have them make a note to remain after the main meeting and move on with your scheduled agenda.

- **Going off-topic.** The current meeting has a specific purpose. Don't lose that focus. There will be things that come up that are important, but not on topic. You may have too many nonessential people there, or you might be missing key stakeholders necessary to solve this issue. Schedule another meeting, or finish the current one and deal with the new issue at the end. Remember to let the folks who don't need to be there get back to work.

- **Going over time.** As a project manager, you expect your team members to be able to estimate the amount of time it will take them to complete a specific task. It will be detrimental to the schedule if they go too far over the budgeted time in your meeting.

- **Meeting too often.** If you are following an agile methodology, quick daily meetings are necessary. If not, be sure the meetings you hold cover information or collect data that couldn't be assembled in another way.

- **Indulging long-winded participants.** As the leader of the meeting, it is your job to use a nonverbal "stop" (hold up the palm of the hand toward the speaker) and smile. Say, "Your point is well taken, but in the interest of time, we are going to need to move on" (or "hear from others," or "come back to this point later if there is time").

As you are the leader on the project, team members may feel they can't speak up about unproductive meetings. So, evaluate your own practices and see if you can improve them on your own.

Chart a Course for Change

Kathy MacDougall
Erie, Colorado, U.S.

NEW SOFTWARE CHANGES THE WAY IN WHICH PEOPLE WORK. This may be good for the organization, but the people who work there aren't always ready to embrace change. And let's face it, if people can't be convinced, cajoled, or commanded to use your new software, it's been a big waste of time and money.

When requiring people to change the ways in which they work, the carrot method (reward) is much better than the stick (punishment). Even if they're forced to adopt it, if your new software does not provide significant benefits that users can understand and master, they will find every way possible to avoid using it. Proper care must be taken to 1) understand the impact of this change on the people it touches, and 2) put in place change-management plans that help these people embrace the change.

Key to understanding the impact of the change is to understand how people currently work and exactly how the new software will change that process. This increases the chances that users will adopt the new system, and also improves the design of your end-product, as it ensures that it will fit user needs.

The importance of change management cannot be underestimated and should be a project manager's focus early on in the project. To determine the impact of the change on users, first document all current ("as is") processes that touch the software project. Create process flow diagrams that detail daily tasks as well as data inputs and outputs.

Next, document how these processes will differ once the new software has been rolled out. Speak frankly with target users of the new software. Discuss how the changes will affect their work. Listen carefully, evaluate the impact and costs of each feature change, and adjust the software design accordingly. Make sure that the changes will be acceptable to target users and their management.

Involve managers of the target user community early and often. They will be important champions of change who can make or break the transition to the new system by incentivizing and/or mandating that end-users make the switch. They are invaluable partners to remove obstacles and solve unforeseen issues with the rollout.

Create a plan for change. Determine the list of training and team-building activities that will need to happen prior to the project launch, and build these into your project schedule. Enlist help from the management community to create the change management plan. At a minimum, this group must buy into the concepts, implementation and training approach, and timelines wholeheartedly. Listen carefully for objections or warnings about approaches that will not work with their teams.

In summary, users and their management are interested in keeping their focus squarely on meeting their business objectives. Transitions to new processes, tools, and systems pose a potential threat to these goals. Solid upfront planning helps provide a smooth transition to the new system, paves the way for buy-in and acceptance, and increases the chances of its long-term use.

IT Program Management: Shared Vision

David Diaz Castillo, MBA, PMP
Panama City, Panama

ORGANIZATIONS OFTEN GROUP SEVERAL RELATED individual technology projects into a larger program. The strategy is to complete these projects in a more cost-effective way and to bring strategic benefits to the organization by avoiding overlap or gaps. However, it is vital that the software project manager convey to the project team members the real business objective that their individual project must achieve, as well as how this team aligns to the other projects. Team members must also understand how the achievement of their specific project goals contributes to the success or failure of the overall program objectives.

Here are some key tasks:

- Find the connections that expand the importance of this project beyond its mere standalone value.

- Define the relationships, deliverables, and risks shared among all projects in the program.

- Keep all the team members in alignment with the final solution that the program is trying to achieve.

- Understand the business, to propose solutions aligned to the strategic objectives of the program as the inevitable problems appear.

This concept of bundling projects into programs is not very mature in Latin America yet, but we are gaining experience managing programs with a common set of governance policies. Clearly there are rich benefits to be found when each team has a clear vision of the entire program goals, not just its own project work.

The most difficult thing is getting the buy-in from vendors, clients, sponsors, and other stakeholders. We need to analyze their interests, requirements, and needs to be sure that there is value for each of them when we group technical projects. Every group must gain more value than if its project was completed in a vacuum.

Particularly when customers span many countries, they will all have different ideas of how technology should be created, and unique organizational procedures and processes. Agreement and approval on internationally recognized program management practices is fundamental in order to begin the alignment of all stakeholders to program goals.

To have a successful methodology, we need common, but flexible, documents or templates to use for all projects. When we manage information technology programs, we typically need goods or services from vendors with their own unique methodology and templates, or outputs from other projects being run simultaneously with our own. So, before we begin, all parties have to agree which documents we are going to use.

What will our project management methodology be? If individual project teams can't agree on what methodology, procedures, processes, and integrated change control steps will be adopted by all teams, the smooth codevelopment of projects to serve the greater program good will fail. When choosing, the software project manager needs to ask the team which templates and practices are reasonable and useful to help it execute and control its projects efficiently.

Once you have a common process and document/template tools, you are in a position to coordinate technical projects into programs. These provide greater value to your customer and your organization than single projects done alone.

Planning for Reality

Craig Letavec, PMP, PgMP, MSP
Waynesville, Ohio, U.S.

IT'S AMAZING HOW OFTEN SOFTWARE PROJECTS tend to fall into late, over-budget, off-quality situations. Even in highly touted software shops with international certifications and maturity assessments lining the walls, the trials of managing the very fluid environment of software development are many.

The pace of development will naturally vary throughout the life of the project. Sometimes you are ahead of schedule, sometimes behind. Often, project managers seek to control these fluctuations through strict, elaborate project timelines that lay out prescribed task assignments and deadlines. However, they find themselves making multiple revisions to the plan along the way to deal with the dynamic nature of creating software.

While the development and execution of a detailed, keenly estimated project plan is important in the success of any project, many software project managers may find some benefit in adding some "reality time" into their plans.

The critical chain method uses the concept of "buffers" as one means to deal with inherent variance over the life cycle of the project. Try introducing "buffer time" or "reality time" into your schedule at each phase of your software development life cycle (design, coding, testing, etc.).

Buffer time allows for a degree of flexibility within a phase without the need to perform major scheduling adjustments. Think of this buffer time as a time contingency reserve for the phase. The process is fairly straightforward. Look at each phase of your project, consider the total duration of the phase based on your best planning, and then add a buffer task at the end of the phase that has a duration of a percentage of the total phase duration, say 10% or so.

For example, on a 40-day total duration for a design phase, add 4 days of buffer time to the end of the phase, for a total phase duration of 44 days. Will the phase actually take 44 days? Perhaps not, but the "unused" time can then be either carried forward or added to future buffers.

As experienced software project managers know, projects may proceed on schedule during the early stages, only to end up dragging on later in the process. Getting ahead of the curve almost always has more advantages than disadvantages.

Expect skepticism the first time you try this approach. "Nonproductive" time is the first thing managers will want to eliminate when they review your schedule. Stand your ground. Make the simple point that you are performing basic schedule risk management.

If you have a phase of the project that is riskier than another, add more buffer at that point. You may be able to add less of a risk buffer in other spots on the timeline.

Last, make sure that you are not "double-dipping." Double-dipping would be adding extra time at the task level and then again at the phase level. The technique works best when you are not already buffering each of your task durations by routinely adding extra time to each activity to deal with the unknown.

Try it. It works!

The Fallacy of
Perfect Execution

David Wood
Fredericksburg, Virginia, U.S.

IF YOU THINK YOU CAN CREATE FLAWLESS CODE if you work hard enough, don't be embarrassed. Many others have thought so, too. Unfortunately, it is not possible. Even in theory.

Arbitrary logic is hard to verify in the general case and hard, or impossible, to fully test. Drawing an analogy to the bricks and beams used in other construction-related activities, three researchers in the UK recently suggested that software is hard to verify because "there are no good, predictable building blocks. The elements out of which programs are constructed: statements, procedures, or objects, cannot be composed in a predictable fashion."

The building blocks of software don't snap together like Legos. They can be put together in so many ways that it is impossible to determine all of the combinations. That may be a decent working definition of Turing completeness.* Software is, in a word, complicated.

Tracing and verifying arbitrary logic in code may sound esoteric. How about the simpler job of tracing programmer intent? Surely we can talk to programmers and ask them what they meant. Unfortunately, programmer intent is generally lost within a few days of writing a code block, especially when requirements change or are inconsistently documented.

Programmers also change jobs, leaving undocumented or wrongly documented code behind. Source code rapidly becomes the last and only forensic clue to programmer intent. Alas, intent can only be imperfectly ascertained from clues like variable names, logic flow, and the occasional comment.

---

* *Turing completeness*: Named after Alan Turing, this is the concept that every design for a computing device could be emulated by a universal machine. True Turing-complete machines are physically impossible, due to the unlimited storage they would require. However, Turing completeness may be attributed to machines that would be universal if they had unlimited storage.

Bugs will remain part of every software product shipped. We put bugs into software for both bad reasons (like ignorance of language features or poor attention to detail) and good ones (such as conflicting or poorly communicated requirements). Further, bugs are a source of change in software because when they are recognized we refactor the code to fix them, injecting new bugs in the process.

Meir (Manny) Lehman was the first to recognize that software evolves during its life cycle, way back in 1969. He later figured out that multiple feedback loops exist within a software development effort, and that those feedback loops influence the process of evolution. They include the injection of multiple (possibly conflicting) requirements and design decisions.

Various degrees of programmer understanding of requirements, design decisions, and implementation details contribute to other feedback loops. In other words, the sources of bugs don't have to be logical programming errors. Bugs are also introduced by differences of opinion.

The Fallacy Of Perfect Execution is the delusion that it is possible to create flawless code with sufficient attention to detail. If that were so, we would all be strong advocates of structured programming techniques. We aren't, and for good reason. Software, at any stage of its evolution, is buggy, extremely likely to change, and inaccurately documented.

That insight, simple though it may be, encourages us to approach software differently. It encourages us to develop tools and techniques to incrementally refactor software implementations, requirements, and documentation.

Introduce a More Agile Communication System

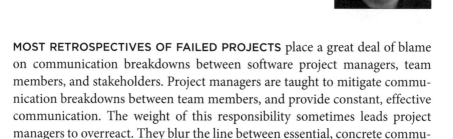

Brian Sam-Bodden
Scottsdale, Arizona, U.S.

MOST RETROSPECTIVES OF FAILED PROJECTS place a great deal of blame on communication breakdowns between software project managers, team members, and stakeholders. Project managers are taught to mitigate communication breakdowns between team members, and provide constant, effective communication. The weight of this responsibility sometimes leads project managers to overreact. They blur the line between essential, concrete communications and those where the content-to-noise ratio actually harms project progress instead of helping it.

To solve this problem, many software development endeavors are moving toward a more flexible, agile process. The key to agile methodologies is timely communication loops that enable agile teams to respond effectively to unforeseen changes, and quickly reassess and reprioritize project features.

How do agile project managers keep communications limited to the essentials? They promote the daily "15-minute stand-up" meeting. It entails developers describing what they've accomplished since the last standup, what they're planning to accomplish "today," and any impediments they foresee in reaching their goals. The negative risk of a stand-up meeting is that it may rely solely on the precision of each developer's self-assessment. The solution? To make stand-up meetings more effective, integrate a task management tool that can show the output of a feature's tests. A tool does not lie about the state of a project's codebase, and testing results are a valuable addition to developer self-assessment. Presenting report data correlating a feature to a set of tests it passed gives a more accurate representation of the state of the feature.

For example, results from a continuous integration tool can paint an objective picture of progress. This reduces the stand-up meeting communication to the essentials: reporting of impediments (hopefully, already caught by the task management tool) and unforeseen developments due to edge cases, integration challenges, and bugs/defects. By reflecting these development "discoveries" through a shared, globally accessible tool, developers gain a greater level of feedback precision. Often, unseen connections between features and tasks can be discovered early.

One typical misconception is that synchronous* communications are always more effective than asynchronous† communications. Adding development tools and short, asynchronous communication loops can effectively supplement face-to-face communications.

At a more general level of feedback, a wiki system can easily keep the vision of the project adjusted to the reality of the development progress. Such a system can also make information available in a timely manner and provide a higher-level channel to communicate to stakeholders-at-large, who might not be interested in the deep, technical details impeding a particular feature's progress. By contrast, a software developer's vision of the overall project can be blurred over time by the minutiae of his daily technical work. A wiki is an effective way to keep a clear, shared vision of the project among all the participants.

By attacking the problem of keeping information loops tight and noise-free, software project managers can help avoid the breakdown in communications typically blamed for project failures. A project manager's responsibility and challenge is to streamline the feedback loops at every level of a project.

---

* *Synchronous communication*: Participants all participate at the same time, whether in person or by virtual means.

† *Asynchronous communication*: Participants have access to information, but do not have to be physically present and available in real time. Examples include email, discussion boards, and shared folders.

Don't Worship a Methodology

Fabio Teixeira de Melo, PMP
Coatzacoalcos, Veracruz, Mexico

MANY PROJECT MANAGERS GET OVERLY INVESTED in following a methodology, which hinders their ability to manage the project to a useful, praiseworthy completion. If you used a certain format in your last job, studied it in school, or obtained a certification in it, you may feel tempted to rigorously establish all the processes and documents your textbook mentions, exactly as they are described. This is a dangerous pitfall and raises the following issues:

- **Required level of effort.** Working thoroughly through all the processes contained in reference materials may require a lot of administrative effort from every team member. Are you sure you have considered all those hours in your time and budget estimates? You certainly don't want to put in place a fantastic set of procedures that document the fact that your project is failing because of the time you took to prepare them.

- **Executing company's culture.** How familiar is your team with those specialized processes? Will you have to train team members? Is that training budgeted? Are they interested? What about functional managers and other company departments with which you will have to deal? Do your processes conflict with formally or informally established company processes and habits? Such conflicts could be a risk to the project.

- **Project focus.** The focus of the project manager must be the successful completion of the project, which in a software project is primarily linked to delivering the software. All the project management knowledge you have at your disposal is a means, not an end. Besides, your team will naturally give importance to the same things you, as a project manager, give importance to. If your focus is the full establishment of, and compliance with, all the project management processes, that will be the focus of your team, too. And then who will create the software?

- **Virtual or geographically distributed team.** If all of your team members are not colocated, it may be very difficult to introduce and enforce mandatory procedures for them to follow. Their hardware and software, as well as other technology, may make compliance with your demands difficult, or even impossible. Narrow your expectations, if necessary, when having remote teams deliver the products or services you need from their small portion of the overall project.

In the end, no project management book or methodology you feel compelled to follow is more important than your good sense. You should go through a product analysis, a contract analysis, a first approach to a risk analysis, and an interview with your major stakeholders (client and sponsor), and then choose your project management strategy.

Try to document it for yourself, with a statement such as "I plan to manage the project this way because…." This will help you adjust your strategy in case the root reasons for your decision change. Based on the needs of the project, you can determine which processes are most important and should be implemented thoroughly, and which processes might deserve a lighter approach. In the end, a good project management plan is all about being effective and keeping it simple.

Don't Throw Spreadsheets at People Issues

Anupam Kundu
New York, New York, U.S.

HAVE YOU EVER BEEN SHOWN A SPREADSHEET with lists of activities to explain your work on a project? Many experienced managers try to use spreadsheet lists as a "silver bullet"* for managing and monitoring projects.

Tom is an information technology development architect in the online division of a large organization. He serves four or more different stakeholder groups. Since he has a poor ability to prioritize the deliverables for different stakeholders, he ends up annoying or disappointing someone every week. With too many commitments to fulfill, and too few resources on hand, he is always at the center of the resulting conflicts among the groups.

Tom and his team are talented IT architects, yet their lack of time and the skill sets necessary to manage stakeholder expectations creates problems for everyone in the online group. The solution? Get a trained software project manager to prioritize and list the deliverables for Tom and his team every week, month, or quarter.

The PM can facilitate discussions with the various stakeholders to prioritize the deliverables. Then, the priorities are evaluated across all the internal customers. This way, not only do the stakeholders have their expectations set correctly, but Tom and his team get a frequently refreshed list of tasks. They can stay focused on developing the most important items on that week's agenda, across all projects.

The secret to making this plan effective is not to stop with a spreadsheet list of deliverables for each project. Instead, the PM sets the expectations of the

---

* *Silver bullet*: In folklore, a silver bullet was the only kind of ammunition that would be effective in killing a werewolf, vampire, witch, or other variety of monster. Now, the metaphor can mean a new software or technology that will magically solve all major organizational problems. It can be any solution that is perceived to have far-reaching effectiveness.

stakeholders by involving them in prioritizing what features or functionalities are the most important/valuable/revenue-producing, given the amount of resources (time, money, and people) at Tom's disposal. Then each group gets feedback regarding how much work it can expect that week, given the needs of other parts of the online division. Communication is the most effective component in planning out the work for Tom's team, especially when the priorities of multiple projects must be established.

Perhaps Tom and his team have had an unfortunate experience with one of the stakeholder groups on a past project. With this approach, the "blacklisted" team can continue to get its work completed until time, or a more proactive intervention, helps heal the wounds from the previous interaction.

In the end, software project management is about managing people and managing the processes in which they are involved. Interpersonal conflicts within a team and between vying organizational groups are very common. Diversity in ideas, goals, values, beliefs, and needs are the primary strength of teams, not weaknesses. However, they inevitably lead to personal conflicts and conflicts over the prioritization of the workflow through the team.

Most conflicts are a threat to productivity and efficiency; resolving them satisfactorily can actually strengthen relationships, foster creative change, and improve results. All conflict resolution tactics depend on proactive communication, active listening, compassionate understanding, and some effective negotiation and/or arbitration. Skilled software project managers are needed—because you can't solve people issues with spreadsheets.

One Deliverable, One Person

Alan Greenblatt
Sudbury, Massachusetts, U.S.

EVERY DELIVERABLE SHOULD HAVE A SINGLE PERSON who is responsible for its completion. Everyone working on the project should clearly understand who is responsible for the delivery of each item. Actual development of the item may involve a large group of people, but ultimate responsibility for ensuring its on-time completion, and for understanding the technical issues surrounding that item, should be associated with one person.

Too often, especially in highly politicized environments, responsibilities are shared, particularly when things are a little fuzzy at the beginning of a project. People like to be responsible for highly visible items that they know are going to be successful. No one wants to be held responsible for something that is sure to be a failure. In the beginning of a project, sometimes responsibilities are shared because a deliverable, and its associated risks, are not fully understood. No one really wants to step up and assume responsibility for a vague task.

Sometimes, a deliverable is so juicy that you end up with multiple people who want to assume responsibility for it. Yet, not wanting to rock the boat, management doesn't assign specific responsibility to one person for fear that others will get upset. Either way, you are setting the stage for much larger problems down the road.

First, if there is a problem associated with a deliverable, one individual who is ultimately responsible for it is much more apt to notify the team early, since she knows she will be held accountable. When time is tight, people have a tendency to assume that anything for which they are not held personally accountable will be handled by someone else. That is how things fall through the cracks. As software project manager, you end up with a crisis on your hands.

Second, as the project moves on, it is simply much more efficient for all team members, especially newcomers, to know exactly who to speak to regarding any issue. If you have a question, you want to make sure you are asking the right person—the expert associated with the topic at hand. And, if the expert doesn't know the answer, he will get it for you. You shouldn't have to spend your time chasing down an answer for something you don't fully understand in the first place.

Finally, sometimes (all right, often), projects don't turn out as expected. If people aren't held accountable for their actions (or inactions), you'll never be able to fix the problems that occur, and group dynamics will suffer. Few issues are more disruptive to team performance than the group wasting time trying to decide who to blame for failure of a "group" assignment.

You don't want to turn this into a contentious means of assigning blame, but rather a means of properly distributing responsibility. And when a deliverable comes in early and under budget (or at least on time and within budget), it's good to know who deserves the praise.

The Fallacy of
Perfect Knowledge

David Wood
Fredericksburg, Virginia, U.S.

WE ALL KNOW IN OUR HEART OF HEARTS that we don't know everything. Every day, hopefully, we learn a bit more about our profession, our society, and ourselves. But we simply can't know it all. If we stop learning we fall behind rapidly, especially in the software industry. The idea that one can apprentice to a trade and practice that trade the rest of one's life has gone the way of the dodo. Remember the dodo bird? No? That's the point.

Technology, techniques, and the ideas upon which they are built change far too rapidly in our era for any practitioner to know all he or she needs to know at any point in time. We must constantly learn and we must equally adjust to a state of ignorance, which requires us to spend some portion of every project researching the knowledge we need. Why, then, do we persist in pretending that we must, or even can, know everything about a software project during its development phase?

The history of software engineering is replete with attempts to control software projects, through carefully bound development and maintenance activities to prevent buggy, failed software. Most such methodologies, such as the classic "waterfall" methodology, presume that with sufficient time and up-front diligence, a software project can be completely understood. Many demand that requirements be set in stone before a line of code is written. What nonsense!

Giving up on knowing it all during development, we might think that we can know it all later. Several software development methodologies presume this, such as the spiral or agile methodologies. Iterative development is seen as the key to delivering a software project encoding "final" requirements. Unfortunately for adherents of those methodologies, delivery of a software project is just a comma in development, not a period.

Requirements, even when "agreed" upon in detailed upfront design, will change during development. It is impossible to know them all in advance. Multiple requirements often result in inconsistencies, even when they are gathered from a single source. Requirements may even mean different things to different people. Differing interpretations may be due to perception, goals, or language. In order to create a successful software project, we must accept and even embrace these ideas. We do not know it all and we never will.

The Fallacy of Perfect Knowledge is the delusion that it is possible to capture complete, nonconflicting requirements for a software project. The reality is that requirements will never be fully known at any time during a software project's life cycle—not during analysis, development, maintenance, or even (or especially) when the system becomes legacy.

Continuous use of the agile techniques of iteration and refactoring into the maintenance phase of the software life cycle begins to address some of these concerns. A fuller understanding of the ways that software evolves may be the next step. Until we have those conceptual tools, use them daily, and accept our ignorances big and small, we will continue to fall victim to the Fallacy of Perfect Knowledge.

Build Teams to Run Marathons, Not Sprints

Naresh Jain
Malad, Mumbai, India

IF YOU RUN AT YOUR FASTEST PACE for a short period of time—a "sprint" in track and field terms—you burn yourself out. To run a marathon, a team must be disciplined, practice every day, and keep a sustainable pace. When working on software projects, we don't want to run just once and exhaust ourselves. We need to keep going at a steady pace. Sustainable teams are geared toward running marathons and not allowed to just sprint.

Building useful software products is not an end in itself. Team members need to learn how to help one another, help other team members realize their true potential, and create an environment that allows everyone to go beyond their limitations.

Most teams have a gap in knowing how to do this. Someone needs to play an active role to fill this void. In most cases, the software project manager is the best choice to work on team development. I suggest the project manager target a goal to build sustainable teams. This is a primary way he/she can add extra value to the project.

If the project manager focuses on team building and individual growth, on-time and within-budget deliveries will automatically fall into place. This also ensures that teams are self-organized and don't need a babysitter if the project manager needs to guide multiple projects simultaneously.

Typically, project managers get caught up in daily fire-fighting tasks. Hence, they don't really have time to strategically build a team. Working with a long-term team development plan ultimately allows the project manager to keep out of micromanagement mode, not only for the current project, but on all future endeavors.

We need a fundamental shift in the focus of software project management practices so that the PM takes a more strategic role. Leave the tactical things to the programming team. This ensures that the team will take ownership of the project and the software project managers can become true facilitators or catalysts, making sure things are moving in the right direction for the project overall.

General George S. Patton said, "No plan survives contact with the enemy." This means project managers need to spend more time empowering their teams to deal with unanticipated changes, rather than trying to get involved in day-to-day coding and architecture decisions. It's foolish for them to think they can fool the information technology team into believing they grasp the intricacies of software development if they do not have a programming background. The team knows immediately that these project managers don't know what they are talking about.

A software project manager is like an operating system's kernel.* The kernel itself does not do end-user tasks, but it ensures that the end-user tasks are correctly completed by the applications sitting on top of it. Similarly, if a project manager can be a true facilitator and coach who ensures optimal collaboration among the team members, it should no longer be an issue to build self-organized teams ready to run marathons and deliver high-quality software.

---

* *System kernel*: The central component of an operating system. It manages the communication between hardware and software and connects the application software—such as Internet browsers, word processors, spreadsheets, and email—to the hardware of a computer. Memory, processing functions, and input/output devices can thus be used by all applications.

The Holy Trinity of Project Management

Paul Waggoner, MBA, PMP, MCSE, CHP, CHSS
Waukee, Iowa, U.S.

THE SOFTWARE PROJECT MANAGER usually defines the role of each team member at the beginning of a new project, documenting why each team member's skills are vital and the general responsibilities each person should anticipate. However, these documents seldom include an explanation of the software project manager's role during the project life cycle.

The challenge for the project manager, especially when working with a new team, is to convey the essence of project management in a 30-minute overview, without overwhelming the team with methodology details.

With a busy organization and team members whose first priority is taking care of their primary work assignment, your challenge as PM is to convey, as concisely as possible, one primary point that team members will take away from your meeting: the "Holy Trinity," also know as the *triple constraint*.

To introduce this core concept, prepare a slide or other visual depicting the triple constraint. This is an equilateral triangle with its three points labeled Time, Cost, and Scope. Together, they outline a space in their center, which is the project Quality. This geometric representation of the project work illustrates that increasing the length of any one of the three sides forces a corresponding change in at least one of the other sides of the triangle. Thus, change also affects the project quality.

Point out that this fixed relationship among the three constraints explains why defining scope becomes a critical first step, and a primary limitation. While you may have your own key points depending on the project management maturity of your organization, the type of project you are helming, the maturity of the project management effort, and past experiences with your customers, be sure to cover these:

- The importance of each team member's individual participation on the project, which includes assisting with the development of the project plan.

- Project risks—what they are, how to identify them, and how to create and monitor plans to avoid, mitigate, or respond to them.

- Tasks needing further breakdown to define the work to be completed by each member of the team.

- Task assignments, scheduled completion dates, interdependencies of the tasks for the entire team, and the project manager's role in following up to ensure timely completion of the assignments.

- Possible task completion delays, impediments to completing tasks in a timely manner, and the PM's role to assist with removing roadblocks.

- Communications plans, team member communication responsibilities, and the PM's role as focal point in coordinating plan details.

- Project status meeting responsibilities and schedules.

- Outline of next steps you plan to perform as PM as the project plan unfolds.

Unless your organization is a "mature" project-oriented business, adding an overview of the basic PM concepts at the beginning of all projects is critical to assist team members in understanding the full extent of their responsibilities and the details of their support structure. This includes laying out your role as their software project manager.

Roadmaps: What Have We Done for You Lately?

Kathy MacDougall
Erie, Colorado, U.S.

GOOD COMMUNICATION INSIDE AND OUTSIDE THE PROJECT TEAM is a key factor in the success of any project. An important communication tool for all projects is the official project roadmap. The project plan helps your immediate project team chart a course for change at the task level. By contrast, the project roadmap allows the broader stakeholder community to understand the change that will happen at a higher level. The project roadmap is a vehicle that helps to communicate the planned changes, the timeframes for specific changes, and the impact these changes will have on the business.

So how does one go about creating a project roadmap? First, enlist the input of top project stakeholders. What features are important to them? What's the priority level of each of these features? Are there things happening within the business that will make it important to have particular features ready by a specific date? Capture the voice of the customer and use this as the foundation for a draft roadmap.

Next, create a draft of the roadmap that shows a list of high-level features grouped into a realistic timeframe (quarterly works well typically). For each feature, describe the business value (e.g., reduce time to place an order by two minutes; reduce cost to place an order by $10) on the roadmap. If the business value cannot be described, you should question the validity of including the feature in the project. In short, items without tangible business value shouldn't appear on your roadmap, and they warrant further scrutiny in the form of a cost/benefit analysis.

Once a good draft has been created, get feedback from the project's executive sponsor as well as from the project stakeholders. Provide a live forum for discussion that allows stakeholders to ask for clarity, voice concerns regarding prioritization, and alert the team to items that are missing from the roadmap. These frank discussions build understanding of the project and help to ensure that the roadmap is in alignment with stakeholder priorities. Adjust the draft according to the input received. Ideally, after completing this step, you'll have a roadmap which is supported by all key stakeholders.

Finally, shout it out loudly—post the roadmap prominently on the project website, present it to secondary stakeholder groups, and use it as a primary communication tool for the projects. Review the roadmap quarterly to make sure you are on track. Tell stakeholders what has been completed and what will be coming during the next quarter. If delays make it necessary to revise the roadmap, go back to the draft stage and repeat. Communicate the newly revised plan to all involved.

This method of creating a project roadmap gives project stakeholders a voice and lets them know what to expect. And last, but by no means least, it affords your team a regular method by which to communicate to others what it has successfully delivered during previous quarters.

The Importance of the Project Scope Statement

Kim Heldman, PMP
Lakewood, Colorado, U.S.

IF THE PROJECT PLAN IS THE HEARTBEAT of a solid project management methodology, the scope statement is the breath. The scope statement details the vision of the project. It describes the goals and deliverables, and documents what a successful conclusion to the project looks like.

Unfortunately, many stakeholders have little interest in going through the exercise of writing a scope statement. Even further, while most project managers do take the time to create a well-rounded scope statement, they often archive it before the signatures are dry and never look at it again. It's important to keep checking back with the scope statement throughout the project to make certain you're delivering what the customer is expecting.

One of my favorite analogies, and I use it often with my customer base, is the remodel story. Imagine you have hired a contractor to finish the basement. The question is, do you give the contractor direction or do you let him decide what the layout will look like? Sure, the contractor will likely have some ideas on layout, how big the rooms should be, and where the plumbing already exists. But what if you want two bedrooms, a three-quarter bath, and a game room, but the contractor builds one bedroom, a full bath, and a family room with a full bar? Not at all close to what you were thinking.

And therein lies the importance of the scope statement. It is the project blueprint. It describes the characteristics of the finished product or service of the project. Without it, you might build one bedroom when your stakeholder is expecting two. The scope statement helps you manage stakeholder expectations. More than once, I have been knee-deep in the project life cycle, usually after a few key deliverables are in prototype stage, and had a stakeholder say, "I thought we were getting two bedrooms." This is where the scope statement comes to the rescue. You certainly don't want to wield it as though it is a weapon, but it is a great way to gently remind your stakeholders what they agreed to back at the beginning of the project.

It's a good idea to periodically review your scope statement with your stakeholders. Project status meetings or steering committee meetings are a logical place to conduct this review. Devote some time every other meeting, or at intervals that make sense given the size and scope of your project, to reviewing the deliverables listed in the scope statement.

If you're conducting regular status meetings, you're likely doing this to some extent already. Status meetings typically address the work accomplished last period, and the anticipated work to be completed during the next work period. Occasionally take the time to go beyond the next work period and remind everyone of the key deliverables that are scheduled to be delivered later in the project.

Regularly reviewing the project scope statement can increase your chances for a successful project and keep your stakeholder's expectations aligned with the goals of the project.

Align Vision and Expected Outcome

David Diaz Castillo, MBA, PMP
Panama City, Panama

SOFTWARE DEVELOPMENT PROJECTS are very challenging, because needs and expectations are not always well defined. The work of a software project manager is to make sure that the following items are in place:

- The main project purpose is well defined.

- Everybody understands why this project is being undertaken.

- The impact for the three Ps (people, processes, and platforms) is clear.

- The needs and expectations are included in the requirements documents. Determine what items are in scope or out of scope, then communicate this to the team.

The software project manager needs to align team members with the vision and the expected outcomes, and master these three additional points:

1. **Business view.** Why is this project the solution? (What problem or opportunity is this project going to solve, or how will this add value to the organization?)

2. **SMART view.** What should the software do? (Make it **S**pecific, **M**easurable, **A**greed upon, **R**ealistic, and possible to do within the **T**ime constraint.)

3. **Subjective view.** What does the end-user think the system will do? (Capture expectations and perceptions from the end-users during the initiating phase.)

Point #1. When coding begins, the programming team and the software project manager focus on the functionality and the technical part of the project, not the main reason that the organization is funding this endeavor.

Future misunderstandings, pitfalls, and errors in the decisions we make happen because the team is not constantly reminded of the real business problem to be solved. The benefits that this project should bring to the organization are not always at the forefront. To avoid this pitfall, the project manager needs to crystallize the purpose, assumptions, constraints, and risks for the project.

Point #2. The technical and functional objective of the project must be clear enough for all team members to grasp, including the project sponsor. The outcomes have to be aligned with the strategic objectives of the business area that eventually will become the owner of the system.

Point #3. The software project manager should identify what end-users expect. How do they think this new application is going to help them in their day-to-day work? The project manager must be clear on these benefits and expectations and communicate them to the development team to get its buy-in. With that clarity, he/she can move forward to convey the advantages accurately to the end-users and help them form a realistic vision of the end software product.

With this detailed grasp of project purpose and benefit, on-the-fly decisions become easier. And, as the software project manager really knows what the users expect and what the system is intended to do, he/she is able to evaluate change control submissions more effectively. This prevents misdirection or tangents occurring during the project execution phase.

We as project managers should discipline ourselves to truly understand both the technical project requirements and the business value the project is intended to provide. With this knowledge, we will be prepared to create better software results and manage uncertainty in a professional way throughout the project life cycle.

Alice Doesn't Live Here Anymore

Barbee Davis, MA, PHR, PMP
Omaha, Nebraska, U.S.

CURRENT DISCUSSIONS AMONG SOFTWARE DEVELOPERS tend to revolve around the best programming language, systems architecture, operating platform, or project methodology. No one seems to notice that one of our team members, Alice, doesn't live here anymore. Where does Alice live now, and how will it affect our software development plans?

She may live in India, where English is often trained phonetically, perhaps by a script. Plan to allow extra time, or use written exchanges, to give Alice the best chance to perform her part of the development, undaunted by the language barrier.

Alice may live in Africa. With a smaller pool of technical talent, people may be more important than projects to her employer. Technology may be limited, so don't assume 24-hour email, phone, and Internet connectivity.

Perhaps Alice has a wonderful job in a developing country. If she doesn't respond right away on conference calls, she may be experiencing a 30-second satellite delay between when you talk and when she hears your words. You'll get the same gap with her answers or comments.

School yourself in the decision-making differences you may encounter with team members from Japan. Anticipate more respect for age and experience. Alice's youth may make it inappropriate or offensive for her to speak up. Japanese team members may also expect group consensus before any information from the meeting is captured in writing.

If you have many Alices in multiple remote locations, you will need to carefully research numerous small issues to allow your team to function smoothly:

- What are the union agreements where Alice works? Are her working hours different? Can she work overtime or weekends, come in early, or work through lunch hours or breaks?

- When do the holidays occur in the country where Alice lives? You'll want to plan any important group meetings with everyone's convenience in mind. You wouldn't ask an American employee to come in on Christmas morning.

- What are the accounting practices in Alice's homeland? Do your reporting cycles coincide with payroll cycles in other places?

- Is there any unexpected data export control? Some places in Europe exert tight control over data transmissions. You may be able to send information to Alice, but can she send you data in return?

- Customer service practices may vary from country to country. If Alice is customer-facing, be sure she knows your team's service standards and quality expectations.

- If you are frustrated by a lack of voice mail, consider that several developing countries feel that it is an automated machine that takes a person's much-needed job. Be respectful when you find cultural differences regarding technology.

- Do you always expect Alice to come in during the middle of the night to accommodate your 9 a.m. meeting every Tuesday? Respect all team members by looking for the least distasteful meeting times, or rotate the unpleasant times among all locations.

We are fortunate to have the brilliant minds and insightful viewpoints of a virtual team. Be sure to use this bounty respectfully.

Avoiding Contract Disputes

Jorge Gelabert, PMP
Berlin, Connecticut, U.S.

PROJECT MANAGERS WHO HAVE BEEN CERTIFIED as Project Management Professionals (PMP)® are familiar with the various types of contracts. They know that the type of contract to use depends not only on the products and services being purchased, but also on the level of risk they and the seller are willing to assume. What they may not always be aware of is that even the best contract does not guarantee that disputes will not arise.

Well-defined requirements are an obvious way of avoiding those possible conflicts. If the contract clearly defines what is expected, both parties will agree on what the deliverables will be. However, well-defined requirements are not always a reality in the world of project management. Some sellers (your sales team) may underbid a proposal with the expectation that the inevitable changes orders from the customer will allow them to recover the profit margin they are losing in order to get the business. Even when projects are bid well and there is a firm, well-defined agreement as to the project scope, changes may arise that both parties must address. These, and any number of other unique scenarios, can become possible areas of dispute.

So what can the project manager do? Approach the project with a mindset that the customer is a partner, not an adversary. If both the seller (you) and buyer (your customer) are invested in the success of the project, disagreements that arise can be easily and amicably resolved. If each side is too focused on its own interests, small disagreements can evolve into major conflicts and derail a project.

When disagreements arise, work to resolve them in such a way that both parties come out as winners. Even when the contract supports your position, negotiate. While you may feel that you would be proven right in a court of law, the damage to the relationship, and the obvious stalemate of the project while the case is being resolved, will impact the ultimate success of the project. While there may be situations when pursuing a legal option is all that is left, it should be a last resort.

The best way to avoid possible conflicts is to be fair when negotiating the contract. For example, if the contract has penalties, make sure it includes bonuses as well. Both parties need to feel they have an equal chance to win and lose. Even with a fixed-price contract, it may be better to renegotiate than to have the buyers (your customers) walk away from the project because they feel they have more to lose by completing the project than by abandoning it.

Also, beware of the bid that feels too good to be true. If your sales team is not presenting a competitive bid, it may mean that your buyers do not fully understand what is required to complete the work of the project. Once they become aware that they are overpaying, they will likely try to renegotiate, or walk away.

You Get What You Measure

Naresh Jain
Malad, Mumbai, India

IT IS A WELL-KNOWN FACT that if you measure the wrong things, you encourage wrong behavior. Software teams suffer daily because their managers are tracking and measuring them against the wrong parameters.

For example, measuring how many hours someone works encourages team members to clock in longer hours. Studies show that working longer hours does not necessarily produce better results. In most cases, it actually results in poorer work quality.

Similarly, measuring and focusing on the team's velocity (amount of functionality completed by the team in a time span) encourages more work to be done faster, but does not necessarily ensure the most important/critical work is being chosen. Therefore, this approach does not solve the real business problem of completing software development both quickly and bug-free.

Focusing on how many bugs the testers report encourages the testers to report more bugs, but not necessarily to report issues with maximum business impact. If developers are measured based on how many bugs are filed against them, testers can become their enemy. This leads to unnecessary team tensions.

In my experience, more software, done faster, does not mean successful software. Rapid software development is good for getting feedback quickly, but building real products needs a lot more than just development speed.

Often when I visit dysfunctional teams, it turns out that the teams were measured using the wrong parameters. Hence the team adapted and optimized itself for those poorly chosen parameters. Lacking the understanding of the project's purpose or vision led to team members defining their own success criteria and measuring themselves against their own respective, disconnected, dysfunctional parameters. Incorrect measurement does more harm than good.

Good project managers ensure that everyone on the team really understands what success means. They help build a common vision and shared understanding within the team. They encourage team collaboration by building win-win situations, so that each team member has the same focus and is working toward the common goals. They help the team identify what really needs to be measured. The secret sauce of successful projects is in using metrics as a means to an end and not as a deliverable in their own right.

I find if I try to measure 10 different things at once, it gets very confusing and distracting for the team. Limiting myself to measuring two or three parameters at a time, however, is very effective. These two to three parameters should be unanimously decided by the team based on current issues hurting the team, or on risks that the team feels will impact it in the near future.

Once the issue is resolved or the risk is mitigated, the team should remove the old checks and replace them with new items added to its metrics. A team that does not periodically change its metrics is symptomatic of a bigger problem.

Be sure that what you are measuring is of value, and know that it may change during the project. You get what you measure, so be sure you are measuring the right things.

Don't Fall into the "Not Invented Here" Syndrome

Dr. Paul Giammalvo, CDT, CCE, MScPM
Jakarta, Indonesia

PROJECT MANAGEMENT is nothing more than a set of processes, and when integrated and combined, these processes result in a methodology. And those processes/methodologies have nearly unlimited application.

There are five sets or groups of processes associated with project management:

- **Initiation.** Those processes that authorize or recognize that a project exists.

- **Planning.** Those processes that enable us to identify what needs to be done and how to go about doing it.

- **Executing.** The actual execution of processes identified in the planning phase to produce results.

- **Monitoring and Controlling.** Those processes where we assess whether the project is progressing in accordance with the plan.

- **Closing.** Those processes that identify whether what we did was done on time, within the allocated budget, and in substantial conformance to the specifications so that the project achieved the results for which it was undertaken.

The information technology sector has been particularly reluctant to look at what others are doing in project management. It doesn't appear to adapt or adopt "best practices" from those sectors that are more advanced or mature in order to increase the success rate of IT projects.

The two great sectors to use as benchmarks are medicine and commercial aircraft piloting. Why? Because both medicine and commercial airline piloting embody project management into their delivery systems. For medicine it is each operation or procedure, and for commercial airline piloting it is each flight from point A to point B. But more importantly from the perspective of IT, the comparative success rate in both medicine and commercial flight is extremely enviable.

So what practices do medicine and commercial aircraft piloting have that IT does not? First, there is the near-total *authority* of the doctor/pilot in making decisions. The flip side of that is people in these positions assume total *accountability*, both financial and professional. In the case of commercial pilots, they risk their own lives if they make a mistake.

Second, neither medicine or commercial piloting accepts "average" practices. PMI's *PMBOK® Guide* states that the project management body of knowledge represents those skills, tools, and techniques that are "generally recognized as *good* practice."

Third, project management as implemented in the fields of medicine and commercial airlines is *not* a standalone methodology. It exists, and is successful, largely because project management is fully and inextricably linked with asset management (departments that are responsible for the allocation and use of organizational assets to fund projects) and operations management (departments that generate revenues for an organization by handling its day-to-day work). Information technology projects cannot be successful in any organization without asset management providing adequate organizational resources, and operations management, as an internal customer, having realistic expectations.

Software project managers need to be willing to look outside their own IT world and learn what has been successful in other applications of project management, especially medicine and commercial airline piloting, which enjoy significantly higher success rates than do IT projects.

Favor the Now
Over the Soon

Scott Davis
Broomfield, Colorado, U.S.

ONE OF MY FAVORITE SAYINGS IS, "Exaggeration is a million times worse than understatement." The project management variation on this is, "Now is a million times better than soon, and a gazillion times better than later."

If you're in the software development industry, you're familiar with the "vaporware" phenomenon—software that is endlessly talked about but never actually delivered. We can plan the software. We can discuss the features it will have. But software that you can touch, run, and interact with is a million times better than a Word document full of requirements.

This means hurry up and write the software—now! The prototype you put together will instantly give you feedback about usability. Worried about performance? How can you optimize performance without the software?

Agile software methodologies favor now, over soon, by focusing on quick iterations. Often they span no more than a week or two. The idea is to get software written and in front of the user as quickly as possible. If users like what they see, you have an immediate victory. More importantly, if they don't like what they see, you have failed fast.

A quick success is only a hundred times better than a late success, but a quick failure is a million times better than a late failure. It gives you time to rethink, readjust, and rewrite the software sooner rather than later. A failure one week before the ship date can be a showstopper. A failure early in the process gets forgotten by the time the software actually goes live.

If the software language or framework that you are using doesn't let you roll out new features in a matter of seconds or minutes, then the tool you are using is part of the problem. If compiling your code takes hours instead of minutes or seconds, you will be less likely to build early and often. These friction points in the software development put you at a distinct competitive disadvantage. Many of the top websites that you use on a daily basis can roll out new features in as little as 30 minutes.

They are also industry leaders because of the quality of the software they produce quickly. They test their code incessantly. Do they wait until the end of the software development life cycle to write their unit and integration tests? Nope. They write them now. Test-first and test-driven methodologies are "de rigeur" in top software development shops, because if testing is important, it is important enough to do now.

It is not that planning isn't a crucial part of successful software projects. Just do your planning based on modern software practices and expectations. Methodologies that date back to a time when code was written out in longhand, meticulously transferred to punch cards, and then hand-carried in a shoebox to a system administrator don't translate well to an era where software is easy, free, and instantaneous. We are in the era of the now, and your processes should be adjusted accordingly.

Speed Is Life; More Is Better

Matt "Boom" Daniel
Coopersburg, Pennsylvania, U.S.

"SPEED IS LIFE; MORE IS BETTER" is a common rallying cry in the jet-fighter community. Imagine the participants, and it is easy to hear, "Gotta go fast!" Right? "Everything must be done with immense speed!" Right? "Get there *now*, get away *now*!" Right?

There is no denying that in the daily flying life of fighter pilots, *speed* is a fundamental *need*. (Mav and Goose said so in the movie *Top Gun*, so it must be true.)

But is it always true that speed is life and more is better?

In a classic one-on-one dogfight* engagement, it is a viable tactic to go very slowly to minimize your turn radius. You turn in a circle with a smaller circumference, forcing your opponent to fly in a larger circle and end up in front of your aircraft so you have a better firing position. You "live inside his circle." This is true control, as both aircraft are flying at the speed of a major league fastball while executing this choreography.

Scientific studies prove the advantage of optimal, rather than excessive, speed for specific moves, tactics, and delivery profiles. Optimal speed, not maximum speed, is the goal. So, once specific needs or tactics are chosen, speed is only a key metric. But more important is how you choose to use that energy (speed).

Venturing outside of the fighter-pilot world to that of business, does the first company to launch a new technology always win? If the goal is to have a survivable, relevant product or service, then the answer is, at best, "maybe."

---

* *Dogfight*: In aviation history, a dogfight is a style of wartime aerial combat where two opposing forces engage in battles in the air. Emerging in World War I, dogfights between two planes were exchanges of gunfire and accompanying avoidance maneuvers.

Being the first to market (speed) may not matter at all in your organization's business plan. The technology world is replete with examples of first-comers who washed out, or fell victim to too much focus on energy (speed), and not enough on energy management (applying that speed only when it served a business function):

- **Communications satellites.** Iridium (a global satellite-phone technology) was outsold by easier, cheaper communication systems that became more accessible to the average person.

- **VCRs (Videocassette recorders).** The Betamax recorder, developed before the Video Home System (VHS), was a superior product that was first to market. The technology became obsolete when the company refused to cross-license its products, services, and spin-offs.

- **PDAs (Personal digital assistants).** Apple Computer's Apple Newton digital assistant, although early to market, was ultimately surpassed in sales by the interactive Palm phones.

- **TV-to-Web.** WebTV was an early, innovative product that used a television for a display rather than a computer monitor. It just never caught on.

Ask yourself, how do you as a software project manager balance speed to release with ensuring long-term relevance? What are the tools or practices you use to make sure that your new solution does not fall victim to obsolescence?

Do you have a "speed is life; more is better" focus? Is it a strength, or is it a weakness? In your environment, what does speed represent? What does energy management mean to your project team?

Building the Morale on Your Team

David Bock
Reston, Virginia, U.S.

A MAJOR ROLE FOR THE SOFTWARE PROJECT MANAGER is to create a work environment that fosters the growth of team morale. Here are some tips to help you start that process:

- Give your team some control over the direction of the project. Do you talk with your team frequently? Do you regularly seek out its input? Can someone make a suggestion, or bring a complaint to you, and feel like you will actively work to effect a change because of it?

- Defend your team against "the bureaucracy." Every organization has its share of rules, and one of your jobs is to apply them in context. "In context" means that, when appropriate, you will defend your team.

  When a corporate memo comes out with rules banning cubicle decorations, will you argue with management so Bill can keep his Rubik's cube collection on display? Even if you lose, the team's morale will benefit.

- Look for ways to improve the work environment. I knew an engineer who worked in a cubicle next to a window. But, according to the company organizational chart, he didn't warrant a window office. Corporate solution? The cubicles were reconfigured so that the window in his workspace was blocked. Rather than argue with the "furniture police," a good manager would be the first person to start moving those cubicle walls to uncover that window.

- Make your team feel like a team. One team had a Player of the Week award that changed hands at the team meeting each week. Russ might say, "I'm giving Mary the team player award because she worked late Thursday night. I was late getting her the documentation, but thanks to her efforts, we still finished the iteration Friday morning." The next week, Mary would recognize another team member's contribution and pass along the award.

- Respect the work-life balance. It is all right to demand overtime from people occasionally, but if you are going to take time from their lives, you need to give some back. Your employees shouldn't be afraid to schedule a morning doctor's appointment or attend a child's afternoon recital, especially after they've worked late to meet a deadline.

- Understand how cause and effect shapes morale. When you merely try to recreate what motivated you or others on past teams, you may be missing the key elements. If you ask yourself, "What can I do to improve working conditions of my team?" and actually work to make those changes, morale will usually improve.

- Make sure your activities are visible. You are a team member, too, so the team should be aware of the work you are doing for it. It is easy to distrust a manager who is always behind a closed door, and easy to follow one who is openly, visibly working for the good of the team.

In your organization there will be unique opportunities to improve morale. Consciously look for them and take advantage of them. If they work, share them with others.

A Project Depends on Teamwork

Lelio Varella, PMP
Tijuca, Rio de Janeiro, Brazil

A PROJECT IS AN ENDEAVOR OF A MULTIDISCIPLINARY NATURE. It can be seen as a collective effort, jointly performed by people of great diversity. Once deployed according to their own unique skills and competencies, and properly coordinated, team members are able to produce major results and fulfill the expectations of the project's stakeholders. If we look to an information technology solution development project, for example, we may identify different participant activity and group categories:

- **Activities.** Business Processes Review, Information Technology Solutions and Services Definition, Products and Services Development, and New Processes and Services Activation.

- **Groups.** Client Business Area Team, Information Technology Department Team, and Outside Service Providers Team.

Project activities are work units requiring the participation of individuals from different groups within the organization, and eventually participants from external organizations, such as vendors and service providers.

These groups are formed by people with different centers of knowledge and competence who, in practice, manage and/or carry out the project activities. The members of each group are usually involved in a set of unique activities within the project.

To work effectively and produce a positive result in the project environment, the allocation of responsibilities should tie directly to individuals and not to the departments or organizations to which people belong. These responsibility assignments should be documented in the project plan.

Depending on their own abilities, and on the nature of the activity, each individual can act simultaneously in various roles during a project. An individual may act as a leader in one situation and a participant in another.

The overall participation and contribution to the project results from each group is measured by the collective sets of activities the group's members complete. Whereas individual responsibilities may be shown in a responsibility matrix, a joint vision of the activities and overall responsibilities of each group participating in the project is necessary as well.

In every project, there are diversities involved, nowhere more obviously than in software development projects. Teamwork depends on two key principles that need to coexist and work together to allow success: delegation and responsibility.

Delegation should follow the pattern documented in the project's work breakdown structure. Split the work to be done. Then split the assignments to get the work done accordingly. This is the only viable way for human beings to understand, execute, and manage really big projects.

To delegate you need to take into consideration the adequate combination of technical and managerial competencies required for each task. Once you've delegated, do not interfere. As the software project manager, you are needed to monitor, give support, and ask about results. In doing so, you will provide motivation, earn respect, and foster team member "response-ability."

"Response-ability" includes taking full responsibility. Remember this when delegating, as well as when accepting assignments. Match the person's skills and abilities to the task.

Once leadership, delegation, and responsibility are in place, each supports the other. Better results are almost guaranteed. And this leads to project success.

Serve Your Team

Karen Gillison
Leesburg, Virginia, U.S.

LONG BEFORE I HEARD OF AN AGILE* METHODOLOGY, I worked with the best project manager I ever met. Looking back, he was using prototype techniques from the agile approach. He viewed his job as a facilitator for the team. He saw his day-to-day duties as identifying and removing obstacles, and providing team resources. He was doing things that increase team velocity.†

There were no multihour meetings where you fight to stay awake until it's your turn to provide a status update—the ones where you wish you could escape and actually write some code, so you will have some progress to report for the next meeting. Instead, we started each project with a kick-off meeting, inviting people with job functions from requirements to testing. The whole team met to get a shared vision and understanding of the project. Then, every few days, the project manager would come by for what we called "doorway" status meetings. Each teammate gave a brief update on what was complete, what was in progress, and what issues were critical.

This project manager tracked project status in a visual, obvious way. He had a master spreadsheet for all the assignments, listing who should complete them. He updated this document regularly, and posted a large printout outside his doorway. Having information posted where we could all see it was great for team communication. An added bonus was that it was also visible to upper-level members of management, and provided them with a self-service way of getting status updates whenever they wanted.

---

* *Agile*: An evolving methodology that promotes a software project management process that encourages shorter planning phases, more adaptability to change, teamwork, unit testing, personal accountability, and frequent customer involvement.

† *Velocity*: A term used in agile software development to show the rate of progress for a team or a team member, i.e., how much an individual programmer will be able to produce in a given time period.

A few words about "ego." My favorite project manager had the maturity and self-discipline to keep his ego out of the way. Even though he was the boss, he didn't abuse his power, change tasks, or shift direction based on a whim. His actions were never detrimental to team productivity, since his main goal was to facilitate the team's progress toward excellence.

By controlling his ego, he and the team achieved amazing results with satisfied end-users and upper management, all while meeting budget and time constraints. Because this management style was so effective, there was a noticeable absence of all-nighters, yelling, and general tension at the end of the project. In less mature corporate environments, a project manager and a smoothly performing team may not be recognized, because every project will seem easy. Even without acknowledgment, satisfaction came to our team members through doing right by the company, the end-users, and one another.

Today, an agile approach can provide new tools to make you a more effective project manager. I suggest you familiarize yourself with them, even if you aren't fortunate enough to work for an organization that has adopted these methodologies. Instead, begin integrating these tools into your traditional project management toolbox. Realize that one of the key roles of the project manager is to increase the team's velocity, and to work towards creating a team environment with few inhibitors to productivity.

The Fallacy of the Big Round Ball

David Wood
Fredericksburg, Virginia, U.S.

PICTURE A BALL, manufactured to be perfectly spherical, perfectly smooth. The only design requirement for this ball is that its diameter be exact when measured at any point. This ball is polished, and polished, and polished some more, until it is perfect. Once no defects can be found, all work on the ball stops. It may not be changed. It is perfection.

Does that sound like any software project you have ever worked on? I didn't think so. Software just doesn't work like that.

Software changes constantly throughout its life cycle. Design decisions, so often based on initial requirements, suddenly seem restrictive when new requirements emerge. Hacks to adapt the code to new requirements violate the design and make the code progressively less maintainable. The ball, however round it was intended to be, becomes battered and bruised.

The Fallacy of the Big Round Ball is the delusion that software system requirements don't change appreciably after delivery or, worse, that they can be controlled.

Early software engineering researchers believed that if requirements could be fully understood before coding began, there would be no maintenance crisis. Some took note of problems created by post-delivery changes to requirements and labeled them evil; static requirements yielded more stable systems. Some sought to limit a user's right to request changes (e.g., "Reduce the need for change maintenance by planning for and controlling user enhancements" was one of a list of "solutions to maintenance" suggested by James Martin and Carma McClure in 1983).

Unfortunately, such strict controls have the unintended side effect of making a software system less useful to its end-users. Such decisions, often based upon short-term economics, were greatly responsible for the alienation of information technology departments from their user bases in the 1990s and the subsequent development of smaller, often duplicate, software systems within business units during that period.

The sands of requirements constantly shift under our feet. Requirements for software projects change for some very good, and very simple, reasons. First, they can. Software is a malleable medium. It is generally much more cost effective to change software than to make equivalent changes to hardware.

Second, users of software most often exist within competitive environments. They compete with one another and with other organizations. As they struggle to compete, they turn to the most malleable parts of their systems for new advantages. Software's flexibility is enticing.

If we give up on the Fallacy of the Big Round Ball, we can become more comfortable with changing requirements and see software malleability for what it is: a huge advantage that we control. Requirements will change. We will have to maintain our code. We will have to inject new requirements that will lead to violations of our designs. That is a feature, as the saying goes, not a bug.

We can design adaptable software, but only if we adapt our thinking first. Adaptability, flexibility of design, and readiness for change should be the cornerstones of any new software project.

Responding to a Crisis

James Graham, PMP
Ta' l-Ibrag, Malta

AT 3:03 P.M. ON JANUARY 15, 2009, Northwest Airlines Flight 1549 lifted off the runway at New York's LaGuardia airport for the short flight to Charlotte, North Carolina.

The Airbus 320, commanded by Captain Chesley Sullenburger III, with 5 crew and 150 passengers onboard, encountered a flock of birds over Brooklyn, New York. Both engines suffered massive damage, causing a loss of thrust, or power.

Listening to the air-traffic audio tapes, two things stand out. First, one can almost hear Sullenburger's brain working as he quickly realizes that the unthinkable has happened. His years of experience and training kick in. Second, one can hear the equally rapid reaction of the air-traffic controller as he continually suggests options to help, in a nonintrusive way.

Over the next few minutes, Sullenburger realizes that his aircraft does not have the potential to reach LaGuardia, Newark, or nearby Teterboro Airport safely, and decides to set down on the Hudson River. It must have been tempting to try to "stretch" the glide to terra firma, but this professional captain weighed the risks of all of his options and chose the one that saw all on board safe.

This is an excellent example of crisis management in action.

Passengers will be comforted to know that airline pilots discuss their actions before every important phase of flight and use checklists that are developed to help them manage both usual and unusual events. This means that they are clear on the vital actions they will take, as a team, during the flight.

This crisis required the crew to work as a team; while Sullenberger was flying the aircraft, First Officer Jeffrey Skyles was attempting to restart the engines to allow a runway landing, and the flight attendants were preparing the passengers to survive the ditching. Each member of the Northwest crew played his/her part in ensuring a good outcome.

When thinking about your software project, consider whether the following conditions are true for your team:

- We have regular team briefings and increase the intensity of these before critical phases (e.g., testing).

- We have a risk register with appropriate responses identified.

- Our risk register is regularly updated and current.

- Our specialists on the team are trained to the appropriate level.

- We have a crisis management plan, with key responsibilities assigned.

- Our crisis management plan has a clear internal and external communications strategy/plan.

If your answers are affirmative, great! You won't have trouble sleeping at night. But if not, then some immediate thinking and planning would be sensible.

Establishing clear responsibilities for dealing with crises is a good start. That is a task that can be done in advance, as can the preparation of checklists, processes, and procedures for each critical project phase. These can be incorporated in the project management plan and its subsidiaries, and communicated so that all the team is clear.

Flight 1549 teaches that a capable team, with well-defined roles, can manage the most challenging crisis successfully.

Know Your Integration Points

Monte Davis, MCSE
Omaha, Nebraska, U.S.

THE HEARTACHE OF EVERY SYSTEMS ADMINISTRATOR, development engineer, and software project manager is systems integration. No matter how promising a newly created application, a freshly purchased software package, or a long-awaited, new-feature-laden upgrade, the business value rests in getting it to work smoothly within the existing company system.

If you are an experienced project manager, but new to the information technology arena, don't let the term *integration* confuse you. Integration simply means linking together all of your various software programs so that all of the subsystems work together to give you more functionality than you could gain from any one application on its own. For example, you want data entry to occur only once and the information to flow smoothly to sales representatives, to accounts payable and receivable, and into other systems that allow various employees to pull up the information they want, regardless of the software interface they open.

Unfortunately, it's often a tense time when new software upgrades are required. They may introduce trouble into a smoothly running process flow. Recently, we had a situation where an upgrade was scheduled for one of our systems. During the upgrade process, the vendor encountered unexpected errors.

There were several views (preprogrammed screens configured to show specific segments of the database information) that were causing the upgrade to fail. The outside vendor doing our upgrade didn't know what the views were being used for, so it deleted them. The rest of the upgrade appeared smooth.

Several days later, a service desk ticket was submitted for a completely separate system that was having issues. Users weren't seeing any new customer data come across from the system that had been upgraded the previous weekend.

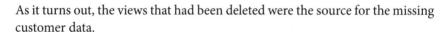

As it turns out, the views that had been deleted were the source for the missing customer data.

Since the source views were deleted to complete the upgrade, the synchronization process between the systems was broken. We had to spend hours troubleshooting the system before we came to the conclusion that the source views were missing. Then we had to recreate the deleted views, by hand, in order to get the two systems talking again.

Most IT departments have diagrams showing how the various components of their hardware systems are connected. But we've found it is equally helpful to have a visual representation of how data flows throughout our organization. Show the crucial junctures where data from one application flows into other programs.

We learned that in situations like this, it helps to have good documentation illustrating where your systems are reliant on one another. When we initially met with the vendor engaged to manage our upgrades, we could have shared our business flow diagram.

The initial upgrade problems could have been solved in another way, rather than deleting crucial views that fed other systems. We could have saved ourselves downtime and administrator stress, and come out of the upgrade process confident that we didn't have to live in fear that other, hidden problems had been introduced to the system.

Aggressively Promote Communication in Distributed Projects

Anupam Kundu
New York, New York, U.S.

DISTRIBUTED PROJECTS CREATE UNUSUAL CHALLENGES since the project team members are not colocated (not physically together). As a result, the following issues can become impediments to the success of a project:

- Lack of trust between the geographically dispersed teams.

- Unwieldy amounts of time spent on communication.

- Inability to foster a "one-team" feeling due to cultural differences.

- Lack of participation from team members during common meetings.

- Lack of identity with the project team, as team members in different geographies may speak different languages and/or have different project practices.

These stumbling blocks have become nightmares for many software project managers facilitating distributed projects. Here are few to-dos to add to your communication arsenal if you are assigned to manage a distributed project:

- Find and document the overlap time between different geographically distributed teams (don't forget Daylight Savings Time).

- Publish the instant messaging (IM) addresses of all the team members (and the best time to reach them).

- Make sure that each key stakeholder has all conference call access details (web and telephone).

- Gather and share the vacation details for different teams on a shared calendar.

- Publish a schedule of daily stand-up meeting between geographically dispersed teams. Stand-up meetings are better than sit-down ones; attendees focus because no one wants to stand for a long time.

- Publish the name and a headshot (photo) of each team member. Identify a back-up contact person for each key role.

- Set up a common location for sharing project artifacts among the teams (documents/reports/templates).

Besides enhancing your communication strategy, there are logistics issues that need to be addressed to promote superior communication among distributed teams:

- Invest in high-quality speakerphones for all locations. When participating in conference calls, assurances of stable phone connectivity between different teams will go a long way toward building camaraderie.

- Place the phone in a spacious room equipped with a large table, as you want to seat people comfortably and perhaps provide food for those participants meeting at unusual hours. Add whiteboards so notes from phone conversations can be jotted down quickly for everyone in the room to view.

- Budget funds for a few team members to travel to other team sites, perhaps during the initiation phase or quality assurance processes.

- Create a project dashboard (use any collaboration tool) for teams to communicate their issues. Share these dashboard images among the teams, whether they use online tools or only have the technology for digital photo sharing.

- Publish the overall goals and targets of the project at a common location for everyone to see, even telecommuters.

- Arrange presentations by business sponsors and insist that key team members from every location participate in these presentations.

As virtual and distributed teams become more common, you can increase your chances of success with innovative communication techniques.

Start with the End in Mind

Luis E. Torres, PMP
San Rafael, Alajuela, Costa Rica

CONGRATULATIONS! You're the project manager of that dream software project that everyone wanted to manage. All the company's expectations are placed on your shoulders. Your instinct tells you to run to your desk and start drafting the project schedule, right? Well, there are a number of things to do first to increase the chances of delivering a successful project. One of those things would be "start with the end in mind."

First, take the statement of work (SOW), the contract, or any documentation that would tell you what the customer wants and needs. Find the difference between "wants" and "needs" (I *want* an SUV, but what I *need* is a smaller vehicle with good gas mileage). Now you're in a better position to combine both and answer questions like "what are we trying to accomplish?", "what would make this project a success for the customer, my company, and for me?", and "what would it take to achieve that success?"

There's a lot more to the answer of this last question than just "a reasonable profit." You want the customer to come back to you, you want the project team members to want to work with you again, and you want to become the beacon of reference-ability.

The right attitude and the right people-management skills are paramount to your success as a project manager. Call a kick-off meeting with your project team members and review the SOW to gain a common understanding of what you must deliver.

Next, define the scope of the project and create the work breakdown structure. Identify the quality parameters you must satisfy. Develop the schedule. Figure out how much money you will need. These elements (scope, quality, duration, and cost) will be the basic ones you should monitor and control, and are the cornerstones of your project plan.

Once you break down your project into manageable pieces, you must identify what characteristics the final product must have to satisfy the project's quality requirements. After you have properly sized your project (scope) and noted what "rules" must be complied with (quality), you will be in a better position to determine how long it will take you to finish it.

To find out how much time you will need to complete the project, you need to determine the duration of each individual task, the dependencies among each of those tasks, the specific constraints, and the resources available to you. Cost comes last in this, since it is usually a function of the work you need to do, and the time and resources you will need to complete that work. For example, if you hire a consultant to perform a specific task, it will not cost you the same amount if that individual is scheduled to work for one week than it will if he or she will be working on your project for, let's say, 10 months. Finally, consider procurement, communications, and human resources.

By starting with the end in mind, you have a much better chance to be successful.

Clear Terms, Long Friendship!

Matteo Becchi, PMP
Arlington, Virginia, U.S.

THE TITLE OF THIS TIP IS FROM AN OLD ITALIAN SAYING: *Patti chiari, amicizia lunga*, which means "Clear terms equal long friendship."

I think this mantra applies to many aspects of project management discipline. On a broader, methodological level, this saying summarizes in my mind the idea behind scope statements, setting goals and deliverables, and creating project definition documents. Really, all project artifacts are geared toward stating upfront the terms and goals the project team is setting out to accomplish.

Now take that concept to the 50,000 foot- (or 15,000-meter) view. Look at the initiation and planning phases of the project life cycle across the nine knowledge areas of the *PMBOK® Guide*, from developing the project charter, scope, work breakdown structure (WBS), schedule, cost estimates, to quality/HR/communication and procurement plans.

Each of these activities underlines the heavy focus we dedicate to planning upfront and communicating the plan to all stakeholders to make sure everyone is on the same page. These are basically measures to ensure smooth sailing on the journey that is the project life cycle.

Second, on the tactical level, when running meetings make sure you build, or simply state and set, clear project meeting guidelines and expectations with your team, such as:

- There will be a specific agenda and a required attendees list prepared ahead of time. With the high salary rates of good software developers, you can quickly go over budget if you waste coding time in meetings.

- Agree that each participant will prepare by gathering information, talking to outside experts, reading relevant publications or research, and consulting old notes or company records, as appropriate. A second meeting with expensive personnel because one teammate did not prepare is inexcusable.

- Arrive at meetings early if you need to plug in a laptop, set up projection equipment, or hook up audio devices for your part of the presentation. If not, come a few minutes early to find a chair, get coffee, and greet other team members.

- Set a "policy" of no communication devices during meetings (BlackBerries, laptops, and cell phones). If you've ever tried to speak while your technically adept software developers text or play games, you know that the programmers are tuning you out.

- Agree to respect other project team members by refraining from running sidebar conversations, interrupting, or talking over someone who is speaking.

Third, create clear contracts with your customers, vendors, and subcontractors. The sales division will focus only on the final product to be delivered and the final price your organization will receive. Be sure it also includes specifics of how changes will be requested and approved, and what the charge for them will be.

Try to set a process for how often and in what format the customer expects to be contacted regarding your project. Will your customers be available for questions? Will they be willing to provide end-users to test software features as the development progresses?

Clear terms equal long friendships—no matter where in the project environment you look.

The Best Estimators: Those Who Do the Work

Joe Zenevitch
New York, New York, U.S.

HAVE YOU BEEN ON A PROJECT where one person creates all the estimates for the work to be done? Has this been a successful approach? My guess is, probably not.

There are three major problems with this approach:

- Unless you are lucky, the developers on the team will not be at the same skill level as the person creating the estimates. So, while the estimates might be accurate if the lead architect were doing all the work, more than likely the developer's pace will vary.

- The risk that one person estimating for the entire team will be incorrect is pretty high. The more people involved in estimating, the better.

- Developers are going to be handed an estimate they must meet. Rarely have I seen a developer who is happy with this approach.

The worst infraction is when you, as the software project manager, decide you are qualified to provide the estimates for the team. You may think that since you are a former developer you can adequately choose the estimates. Even if you are still actively doing development, think again. The same issues apply as with the lead architect scenario described above, but the longer it's been since you've done active development, the worse your estimates are going to be. And don't even think about estimating if you are leading a team using a technology with which you are unfamiliar.

On our projects, we do group estimation using a wideband-delphi approach. We start by having our business analyst describe the requirements for a feature, the development team listens, and then team members ask clarifying questions.

Once they are ready to give their initial estimate, they each write their individual figure on a card. When everyone has finished, on the count of three they all hold up their cards.

Now we see how they compare. If they are very close, we go with the more conservative number. If there is a wide discrepancy, we ask the developers to talk about the assumptions that went into their estimate. After more discussion, we ask them to estimate again. What happens most frequently is that the estimates converge to a single number as the developers gain a common understanding and agreement on what will be required to complete the feature.

This approach is advantageous because:

- All of the team is involved in coming up with the estimates and all varying perspectives are shared. Often team members are all of one mind and can get to a shared estimate quickly.

- Later, when actual coding begins, developers have all been exposed to the thought process that went into the estimates, making it less necessary that only certain people can work on any single feature.

- By having the team "own" the estimate, there is less chance of backlash. Their estimate may still be wrong, but team members will be less confrontational about it and more cooperative in coming to a revised estimate.

Remember, the best estimators are those who will do the work.

Communicating Is Key

Gennady Mironov, CPM
Toronto, Ontario, Canada

THE MOST CRITICAL KNOWLEDGE the project manager in any industry should have is how to be a good communicator. The person may have many different certifications and a list of titles and accreditations after his/her name, but without the basic knowledge of how to collaborate with others, the work of the project cannot be accomplished properly.

I strongly believe that when starting a new project, the good project manager should meet in person with all of the stakeholders. Especially the client. The PM should introduce him-/herself and discuss the project goals and all the critical issues. If the stakeholders, client, and even the project team are not located on different continents, meeting in person should not be a big problem, even during an economic recession.

We say in Russia that "it's better to see it one time than to hear it a hundred times." From my own project management experience working on multimillion-dollar projects, I've found I could easily solve problems with my clients within half a day by visiting them in person.

On one project, we had a problem when our contractor was delaying the project schedule by not supplying us with the required wireless base station. The problem was that the contractor had outsourced this part of the project to its own subcontractor, who was late with the power supply systems. Although we spent weeks of calling and sending numerous emails back and fourth, we could not solve this problem.

Finally, I chose to meet personally with our contractor, explained the details of the issue, offered some possible solutions, and we were able to get our needed equipment. In most cases, the customer is on your side and ready to support you if you are willing to listen and help come up with a reasonable solution.

Another time, one of our clients insisted on a very short project schedule. He wanted to shorten the production cycle of the equipment at the end of the year, when all the factories were working at 100% capacity to close as many purchase orders as possible. We could not accept this, because it was twice as short as the standard project period.

Again, I organized a three-party meeting between our company, the client, and the vendor. We freely proposed the shortest, most realistic schedule, and explained in detail why we couldn't shorten it more. After finishing a specially organized inventory to discover the number of items needed for the project we already had in stock, we took some risk and accepted the customer's order without even receiving the order confirmation from him.

We closed the project successfully, two days ahead of that very tight schedule. Our client was very happy, and at the beginning of the new year offered us another unexpected project for another $2 million. We met schedule, scope, budget, and quality requirements, and in this case earned extra profit for the organization as a result of the project.

Software projects rest on person-to-person communication.

A Project Is the Pursuit of a Solution

Cynthia A. Berg, PhD (ABD), PMP
Glendale, Arizona, U.S.

AUTHOR STEPHEN COVEY STATES, "BEGIN WITH THE END IN MIND." And what is a project, except the pursuit of an end solution? The best way to conceptualize the end of a software project is to create a work breakdown structure (WBS). The WBS is a hierarchical view, which shows the entire scope of the project broken down into deliverables,* much like an organizational chart shows company divisions broken into departments and then work teams. The deliverables are then divided into smaller and smaller components until they get to the work package† level.

Include the team, sponsors, and other stakeholders when creating a WBS. This ensures that the work of the project is fully defined and represents the needs of all of the participants. Why include the team? Well, who knows the work that needs to be done better than the project team members who will actually do those tasks? Projects are doomed to fail when the project manager assumes that he/she alone knows how to list every facet of the work of the project.

While creating a WBS, the team has an opportunity to challenge the norms of "how we've always done it." Plus, team members are formulating a shared opinion on what constitutes the work of the project. This method ensures that they will have more buy-in for the effort. After all, it's always more interesting to work on a project you helped to design.

How small should the activities of the WBS be broken down? That's a trick question. There are no activities shown in the WBS, since it is only divided to the work package level. Once that work package is assigned to the department, group, vendor, or subcontractor who will complete it, it can be broken down

---

* *Deliverable*: A product, result, or capability to perform a service that is created through the work of a project.

† *Work package*: The smallest portion of a deliverable, including activities and schedule milestones. The goal is to be able to assign it to one person, group, or vendor.

further into the activities and milestones necessary to ensure that it is done efficiently and with quality processes. Each assignee for a work package, the lowest level of work, should create his or her own smaller project plan portion that will flow back into the master schedule.

The WBS then becomes the backbone for all other planning, executing, monitoring, and controlling functions within the project. It also serves as a succinct communication tool for those both internal and external to the project. A graphic representation of a WBS is a picture of the project solution. Once that picture is completed, the detailed planning, scheduling, and budgeting can begin. How can you plan, budget, and schedule before you have clearly defined the work of the project?

The WBS is also invaluable as a brainstorming tool. With a graphic representation that displays the entirety of the project, it's easy to spot omissions, redundancies, or fertile pockets of work that could easily be enhanced to leverage the value of the project. To identify potential risks (both internal and external), look at each portion of the WBS.

A little time up front to get a clear work breakdown structure that is prepared, understood, and agreed upon among all stakeholders is a recipe for project excellence.

It's the People, Stupid

Adrian Wible
New York, New York, U.S.

NEVER LOSE SIGHT OF THE FACT that the members of your project team are human beings, with aspirations, strengths, constraints, and weaknesses. Your project's success hinges more on team members' attitudes and aptitudes than it does on your Gantt chart wizardry and project tracking prowess. Feel free to manage the project, but don't forget to lead the team.

Many of us manage projects in a matrix environment with team members reporting both to us and to a department manager. We do not have human resources (HR) hiring/firing/evaluation responsibility for them. However, don't abdicate responsibility for the care and feeding of the people on the team to managers in the HR or functional hierarchy.

Many of those managers get promoted based on technical knowledge of human resources or their departments, not on their ability to inspire people. Your project's success depends on your ability to lead. There are many books available on leadership. Read voraciously.

Everyone on your team wants to contribute, learn, and achieve. It may be challenging at times to dig deeply enough to find this desire in some team members, but it's what makes software project management challenging and fun.

Hold one-on-one conversations with your team members regularly. Determine what their issues are, ask them for ideas, and give them a voice in the project. Take their input seriously and act on it.

Ask your team members what they want to be when they grow up. Seriously. We all have career aspirations. Be the one mentor who cares about their careers. You'll be amazed at how powerful this can be.

Be open, honest, and direct with team members. Provide feedback on a regular basis, not just at review time. Focus your feedback on the behavior, not the person. Again, management literature abounds. Study.

When you have a performance issue with a team member, apply the CRAM model: Constraints, Resources, Aptitude, and Motivation. Project managers frequently diagnose poor performance as a motivation problem. The CRAM model suggests that motivation is the last issue to consider. A team member may be experiencing constraints in his life that limit his effectiveness. Examples include getting divorced or married, having kids, fighting addiction issues, etc.

Team members may not have the resources necessary to contribute at their highest level. Examples include no quality assurance (QA) test environment, or ancient hardware. Perhaps budget constraints limit the ability to establish testing environments or buy licenses for necessary software. Perhaps the domain expertise (business analyst, customer, end-user) is not accessible.

Your team member may not be cut out for the role he/she fills. He may not have the programming aptitude necessary for this project. If so, find another project role, if possible. Alternatively, find another team where he can leverage his strengths.

Motivation is the last lever to jiggle when a team member has performance issues. It should only be considered once the constraints, resources, and aptitude problems have been addressed.

Be a leader and connect with the individual human beings who comprise your team. The results may surprise you.

Documents Are a Means, Not an End

Patrick Kua
London, UK

EISENHOWER ONCE SAID, "PLANS ARE WORTHLESS. Planning is essential." Successful project managers understand how to reap the benefits from planning without the overhead of meticulously updating their plans in minute detail. They actively use documents to help spark meaningful conversations, not as the replacement for all communication methods, or worse yet, as a way of pointing out when people breach an agreement.

Planning and tracking will remain essential activities for a project manager, though always framed in the context of achieving a particular goal. Many organizations (incorrectly) measure project managers on how well they stick to a plan, or how thoroughly a particular set of documents has been completed, distributed, and archived.

In organizations that misunderstand planning, project managers are asked, "How accurately did you meet the plan?" Beware of enterprises that ask this micromanagement-centered question instead of the more important question, "Did you deliver the most value in the desired timeframe?" Value may be judged as achieving the right goal within a given budget, delighting customers, or exceeding expectations. With the wrong yardstick in hand, sometimes it's all too easy to forget what the end goal truly is intended to be.

Focusing on just developing plans and the perfect set of documents creates a false sense of progress and accomplishment. It implies that the execution of the plan is the easy part and that the plans are accurate, both of which are hardly ever the case.

I have seen project managers try to force everyone participating in the project to keep to the activities and schedule recorded in the original plan. They fail to realize that, as they recognize changing conditions, it would be more useful to lead the team in replanning activities based on the new circumstances.

Plans and documents contain essential information for a business to meet its goals. However, the plans and documents by themselves are actually quite useless. They need people to act upon the results they highlight and for someone to convey the information they contain to other parties who would then benefit from the knowledge.

Therefore, it is always important to consider what is the right level of information to be passed on and what is the best method for delivering the information to other parties concerned with the outcome of this project. Documents are often the poorest choices to convey important data. The richest level of communication is face-to-face.

Project managers also have the unenviable job of maintaining the delicate balance between the overhead need to meet traceability or auditing requirements and other non-document-centric activities that ultimately add value to a project.

Successful project managers do just enough planning, capture just enough detail, realize that issues will invariably arise as the project progresses, and recognize when plans need to change because of new or unanticipated needs. They remember that the documents from the planning process are the means to a well-run project, not an end in and of themselves.

Can Earned Value and Velocity Coexist on Reports?

Barbee Davis, MA, PHR, PMP
Omaha, Nebraska, U.S.

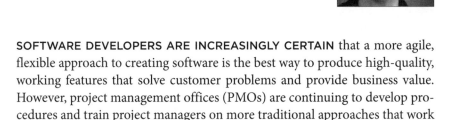

SOFTWARE DEVELOPERS ARE INCREASINGLY CERTAIN that a more agile, flexible approach to creating software is the best way to produce high-quality, working features that solve customer problems and provide business value. However, project management offices (PMOs) are continuing to develop procedures and train project managers on more traditional approaches that work successfully in many non–information technology areas of the corporation.

Is there a way to blend the reporting between the two factions, so that upper management can have matching metrics from both areas? Yes. Sort of.

If you are new to *earned value*, it is a numeric tracking of progress and the business value of that progress on a weekly, monthly, or quarterly basis. In an over-simplistic explanation, ignoring the cost factors, the project manager (and other stakeholders) define requirements and estimate the amount of time it will take to do the work of the project. These estimates are converted into a schedule.

Let's say the reporting time period was one week and the project team estimated it could do 40 predefined tasks in that week. Friday afternoon, the team reports its actual progress. If it got all the tasks finished in those 40 hours, it "earned" 40 hours worth of value (EV). It had estimated, or planned, 40 hours' worth of value (PV). EV–PV=SV, or *schedule variance*. In this case, the team had zero schedule variance.

However, if the team got behind, the schedule would be behind and other workers down the line would need to be alerted. If the team finished early, the original estimates might be excessive, and incoming materials or other project participants would need to know that their tasks may start earlier than anticipated. Remember, the scope (work) of the project has already been set.

The agile term *velocity* means measuring the productivity of a developer. It is used to allow that person to undertake an estimated amount of work for an upcoming week, not to exceed the amount of work s/he completed last week. However, since this developer is only being compared to himself and his last week's choices, rather than a long-term schedule, there is no need to reschedule the work of others. Further, the tasks for this week may be easier, have fewer bugs, or be more familiar to the programmer.

In the software development project, the functionality of the end product has not been set in stone. So if the velocity isn't as fast as originally estimated, the scope (amount of features delivered) can shrink.

The software project manager who is rolling reports from the software development project in with marketing, manufacturing, and training issues needs a reporting metric. The simplest approach is to give information technology a block of time (and a corresponding payroll amount) to work on the software. On the reports, show five weeks of time, for example. When your IT team submits weekly software reports, have it also submit the features/stories completed for you to convert to task names and enter into the report after the fact. Now those tasks can be updated to show that they are 100% complete as planned. This allows traditional reports to show agile progress.

Scope Change Happens; Get Used to It

Pavel Simsa, PMP
Bellevue, Washington, U.S.

IF THERE IS ONE THING that distinguishes a software development project from other project types, it is how, inevitably, scope changes occur. Not that it never happens in other places, but I can't think of another industry with such a constantly fluctuating scope.

You know projects are governed by the triple constraint: cost, time, and scope:

- **Cost.** If your project is in trouble, throwing in extra money or resources rarely helps. If you double the number of diggers, you'll probably get your trench dug in just slightly more than half the time. But if you double the number of software developers, hoping to get the project back on track, it will probably do more harm than good. You will create huge confusion over who owns what code and how things need to be done. So cost needs to stay the same.

- **Time.** There's always "The Date." It is not the delivery date indicated in your original schedule. Nobody officially mentions it out loud, but if you are developing a big security product that is scheduled to release in November, there is a likely chance you will get to keep your job even if your delivery slips until January. Secretly, the team knows "The Date" is February, for example, "at the time of the international Black Hat security conference where new releases are announced." You have some flexibility surrounding your delivery time, but only a small amount. Time is constrained.

- **Scope.** What remains to change is the scope. Oddly enough, scope is one of the most flexible constraints, especially when developing commercial software, rather than software built and customized for a specific customer. The reason is simple. Every new software product has "must have" and "nice to have" features and functionality. The "nice to have" features typically outnumber the "must have" features several times over.

Fortunately, the "nice to have" items are also the easiest to eliminate. If you are building a skyscraper, you can't announce in the middle of the project, "In order to get this project back on track, we'll only build 40 stories on this building, rather than the 60 stories the architectural plans show. We can add the other 20 later, when we have the time."

With software, it's relatively easy to say, "Change of plans—we'll support only two operating systems in Release One. Later, we can add the other two we originally planned to support."

It's not an ideal solution, so what can be done to avoid it? Honestly speaking, probably nothing. It's the nature of software development projects. However, what you can do is to plan your scope concretely. Identify the "nice to have" features and their dependencies from the beginning. The dependencies are important. Removing a "nice to have" feature may otherwise also change the development architectures linked to a "must have."

If you plan possible scope reductions from the beginning, it will make your decision about what to cut and how to cut it easier, should it become necessary.

Buying Ready-Made Software

Ernani Marques da Silva, MBA, PMP, PgMP
Mairipora, Sao Paulo, Brazil

CURRENTLY, IT IS VERY COMMON AND USEFUL to buy software that is ready-made—ready to be tested, implemented, and used out of the box. Why? Such software allows organizations to leverage their efficiency and optimize their effectiveness by cutting time spent in the developmental and implementation phases. In this kind of purchase, you are not only buying the software, but the know-how of the company that wrote the software.

Of course, each organization has its own procedures, policies, and legacy software (e.g., accounting systems, security software, etc.). Therefore, new software often has to be customized in order to support the company policies and procedures, and to integrate the programs with previously installed legacy systems. In many cases, the vendor will capture the knowledge for that customization during the presales process.

This is the point where the major problems may arise. Even if you follow a very detailed procurement process, it is very complicated to determine whether certain functionalities (e.g., formulas, data entry screens, integration with legacy software, etc.) inherent in the new application will work as business/product area requirements intended. Once the procurement process is complete, the contract is signed, and the project plan is approved and in implementation, issues can pop up during the testing phase. The troubles can be related to the customization or, in the worst-case scenario, related to the functionality that the software was assumed to have based on the demo.

It is very important to follow specific steps before the contract is signed:

1. Prepare a very detailed checklist regarding the company's software needs.

2. Visit the company and prepare a due diligence report.

3. Prepare a vendor evaluation report, test cases, and test plan.

4. Make sure the test case is completed and documented.

5. Follow the test plan/cases before the contract is signed.

The gaps, and the plan by which these gaps will be bridged, should be understood and approved by both companies. After this process is carefully followed and documented, you will have very clear information by which to determine which software should be purchased, the estimated time required for software customization, and the actual associated costs. You will save money and time in the long run.

It sounds as if a lot of time will be spent before the vendor is selected and the contract is signed. Yes, but it is better to invest this time rather than waiting until the software is in your hands to be installed. If too many incompatibilities are discovered during testing—or, worst-case scenario, after the software is already deployed to the final user—costs will skyrocket.

To recap, when your company decides to buy ready-made software, spend more time identifying the real need and researching the functional and technical details of the software chosen before purchasing. Use this approach whether the software provider is well known or new to you, and whether the software is a low-impact desktop application or a more crucial server-side application that could bring the company to its knees.

Project Sponsors— Good, Bad, and Ugly

Jorge Gelabert, PMP
Berlin, Connecticut, U.S.

EVERY PROJECT NEEDS A SPONSOR—usually the person who initiated the project and is responsible for providing the financial resources to successfully complete it. Typically, this is someone high in the organization who will champion the project and step in when the software project manager faces company challenges beyond his control. The larger the project, the greater the importance of a strong sponsor.

In my experience, sponsors come in three flavors: good, bad, and ugly. It is important to recognize each type and know how to deal with it.

The worst type of sponsorship is "ugly." These sponsors are usually assigned. Therefore, they have no personal investment in what the project is delivering or its intended use. Such a sponsor tends not to listen to the project manager and instead focuses on arbitrary due dates set by those who have assigned him/her to the project. Benign neglect is common. Assigned project sponsors may change frequently, so there is no continuity.

Spotting this type of sponsorship is easy; addressing the problem is not. The software project manager must work with the sponsor and respond to his/her desires. Often this is at odds with making the project successful. One answer can be to find a surrogate sponsor, a person or group who will benefit from the deliverables of the project and who may be able to provide the assistance typically provided by a sponsor. Alternately, the project manager can ask others with influence to intervene on their behalf with the current sponsor. Your success will depend heavily on how well you, the project manager, are networked within the organization.

The "bad" sponsor can hinder a project in different ways. He or she may become involved in routine matters typically handled by the project manager, interact directly with team members, and make inappropriate project decisions—usurping the role of project manager and confusing the team. He/she may be a weak sponsor, fail to provide needed resources, become overburdened with other efforts, or not have time to provide guidance for the project.

Prevent "bad" sponsor problems by developing clearly defined sponsor roles and responsibilities up front. In the case of the intrusive sponsors, providing them a "job description" of their role may get them to modify their behavior. With weak sponsors, knowing what is expected may make them realize they can't fulfill that role, and you may get a better sponsor assigned to the project.

The ideal situation is having a "good" sponsor. Good sponsors understand their role and responsibilities and behave accordingly. These are the project champions who provide resources, assist when needed, and support the project manager in his/her decisions. It's a company executive who is personally invested in the project success.

Whether "good," "bad," or "ugly," it is your responsibility as software project manager to manage the sponsor, just as you manage the project. Keep the sponsor well informed, involve him/her only when necessary, and avoid allowing the sponsor to take control of the project. Learn to recognize the sponsor types and prepare accordingly.

Should You Under-Promise, or Over-Deliver?

Joe Zenevitch
New York, New York, U.S.

AT THE END OF THE PROJECT, deliver less than you said you would, and you are a bad software project manager. Deliver more than you said you would, and you're the hero. Actually, you should strive to deliver exactly what you promised. No more, no less.

New project managers, eager to please, let business people/customers continue to add features, even as the team's capacity to deliver them shrinks. The business people, thinking that the project manager has things under control, take advantage of this opening, and the onslaught of new features continues.

Afraid to show weakness, the green PMs just sweat it out and hope they can deliver. But as the project end date draws near, it may become obvious that the features list will not be finished. The process of cutting features, not necessarily the newest additions, grudgingly begins. The formerly happy business people are now planning the termination, or at least the post-release punishment, of the project manager.

The experienced PMs know that they are going to have to be firm from day one. Anything that resembles a new feature, or a change in scope, will be met with pushback from the PM. He/she reminds the business owners that only so many features will fit into each release.* If something new comes up, it must be deferred to a future release or substituted for a planned feature.

The experienced PM avoids "High–Medium–Low" categorizations, as customers may mark everything a "High." They prefer a prioritized list of features based on business value. A good PM reminds the business owners that features

---

* *Release*: At the end of a predefined work period, one or more iterations, the goal is to have the feature(s)—working code—of the software available for demonstration to the customer, or perhaps for actual use by a limited user group. This delivery of completed features is called a *release* in agile programming.

at the bottom of the priority list may not get done this release if delays are encountered. These rules serve as an annoyance to the business owners, especially those who haven't learned that ramming in features won't work. Over time, they get used to the process and come to accept it as a fact of project life.

Of course, the experienced PM expects that changes are going to happen during the course of the project, and has built contingency time into the plan. This contingency is held close to the vest, sometimes not being revealed to the customer or even the team. It is managed like a precious resource, and only features that survive the pushback battle get to eat into it.

When this does happen, the business owner is usually thankful that the PM finally obliged him. In the final days of development, if contingency remains, the PM might even opt to "open the reserves" and produce a few extra features. Some business owners might question why they couldn't have them earlier, but in most cases they are happy to receive a few extra, unexpected things.

Now the PM stands at the end of the release. The team has delivered on what it said it would. Sometimes it has provided extras. The business owner is happy, the team is happy, and the PM's reputation is intact. Let the end-of-release festivities begin.

Every Project Manager Is a Contract Administrator

Fabio Teixeira de Melo, PMP
Coatzacoalcos, Veracruz, Mexico

AS THE PROJECT MANAGER, you are responsible for change control. You put together a process for documenting requests and performing the changes. But how can you control changes when you are not aware that they happened?

The client's team members will have direct contact with their peers in your team. Trying to satisfy the client, or being unaware of contractual obligations, a team member can agree to an extra training session, or even implement a change to the software, and forget to inform you—or alert you when it is too late. Some of those changes may be innocuous, but others could bring problems. For instance, silently altering part of the software features means the change may remain unmentioned in the software manual. This could lead to rewrites, reprinting, etc., with all the associated (an unbilled) time and cost.

One might feel tempted to prohibit interaction between members of the client's and the contractor's project teams, but that can jeopardize communication. Contracts don't cover whether or not the client has the right to talk to your team members. And how can a project manager control whether the team members and the client are in contact?

To avoid undocumented changes being performed, every team member should be familiar with the contract, including aspects of scope, time, and each party's rights and dues. They should be prepared to analyze the client's requests when preparing a contract perspective and know how to alert everyone to future changes. This requires that the change control and handling process be documented, and that team members be familiar with it.

A workshop is a very effective tool to provide team members with knowledge about the most important contract aspects and the change control process. Hold this training at the very beginning. Alternately, you may want to include a session about the subject in your internal kick-off meeting agenda. Either way, you should make sure that every project team member is informed.

Special attention must be given to third parties working for the project, such as providers, suppliers, or subcontractors. Controlling the client's access to them is difficult and delicate, and in some cases they may have an independent business relationship with your client. It is not uncommon to see a subcontractor accept a client's request, perform it, and send the bill to you, the main contractor.

The best way to deal with this kind of problem is to avoid it. Talk to your providers and suggest that they inform people involved in your project about the contractual aspects of your relationship both with them and with the client. And introduce them to your change control process.

Remember: the success of a project is measured primarily by client satisfaction. The point is not to deny changes, but to control them. All your team members have to do about this is to detect a potential change and inform you through your change control process. This allows you to control the relationship with the client and to satisfy their needs without sacrificing time and cost.

Important, but Not Urgent

Alex Miller
Ballwin, Missouri, U.S.

THE PERSONAL PRODUCTIVITY CLASSIC *The 7 Habits of Highly Effective People*, by Stephen Covey (Free Press), categorizes activities along a vertical axis, importance, and a horizontal axis, urgency. We now have four possible combinations:

1. Important and Urgent: Velociraptor* attack.

2. Important, but Not Urgent: Preparing future product strategy; reworking a problematic part of the product.

3. Not Important, but Urgent: Neighbor calling to borrow some sugar.

4. Not Important, and Not Urgent: YouTube; surfing the Web.

Let's examine how to maximize our effectiveness.

Consider the Not Important, Not Urgent tasks (#4) first. Most of these activities (the ones you might categorize as "slacking off") can simply be dropped. These activities are, by definition, not important (so why are you doing them?) and not urgent (so they can surely wait). If category 4 activities are mandated by your company, you should be asking your boss why you must do them. Smart managers don't want people doing unimportant work.

We should also strive to reduce the occurrence of Not Important, but Urgent activities (#3). One technique is to ask the source of the event to contact you in a way that lets you deal with the event at a time of your choosing. Another technique is to alter your environment to avoid being interrupted. Phone calls and email are often treated as urgent, regardless of their importance. Use voice mail or email filters to reduce the urgency of these tools.

---

* *Velociraptor*: A small, carnivorous dinosaur characterized as a great threat to humans in Steven Spielberg's science fiction thriller *Jurassic Park*.

Important and Urgent activities (#1) generally must be handled as they occur. However, you should work to install systems (risk prevention) that address the cause of these events. For example, if bugs are causing a system to fail in production, you should analyze the cause of these bugs and institute quality controls to prevent them from occurring again. The best way to reduce the important and urgent events is to institute feedback loops that address the root cause of these occurrences.

The Important, but Not Urgent activities (#2) are the most important things you can do in your job. This is where you do knowledge work and produce value. If you did 25% more of these activities, your boss would give you a raise.

As a software project manager, you are in a unique position to focus the work of your entire team on the Important, but Not Urgent activities. Your job is to buffer your team from meaningless tasks (#4) and Urgent, but Not Important, requests from other teams (#3). You, as the manager, have the power to say no to these requests. Do them yourself, hire a lackey to do them, or just say no!

Your team can't ignore Important and Urgent activities (#1), but if your team spends all its time fighting fires, then you need to fix the faulty wires causing those fires (#2). You might not see the benefits immediately, but over time your team will spend more and more time doing the Important, but Not Urgent, activities that make or break a project.

Teach the Process

Richard Sheridan
Ann Arbor, Michigan, U.S.

FOR A PROCESS TO BE TRULY EFFECTIVE there must be a common understanding of the process among all stakeholders. One of the ways we make sure this happens at my organization is to teach formal classes in our processes to all stakeholders involved in a project. The stakeholders include the project sponsors, perhaps some key users, the project managers, the developers, the designers, and the quality assurance specialists. And, we teach them the process *together* in the same class setting.

We require our clients to take a class in our process during the course of their project. The reason? We want to ensure that the sponsors of the project understand how to steer the team in an effective manner. We combat unrealistic expectations with a commonly understood agile process that incorporates weekly estimating, planning, and show and tell.

Sponsors are taught our estimating practice so that they know how to treat our estimates (estimates are *not* fixed-price bids). They are taught a simple planning technique that chooses scope based on these estimates and is cross-checked with business value. They actively participate in weekly "Show and Tells," which ensure that misunderstandings are exposed as quickly as possible.

Once, I was teaching a class in our process and I called on two of our developers in the class to explain the rules of accountability around estimating. I stated, "Ted and Kealy, you will *never* be punished at this company for missing an estimate." I then turned to our project manager in the class and said, "Lisa, you understand that you are not to pressure or punish our developers if they miss their estimates." I then faced the paying client in the room and explained, "And Jen, you understand that if we go over our estimate, you will pay more for the work?"

Of course, at this point, I have two developers who think I'm tricking them and a client who's ready to cancel the project! I then explain the last "rule" of accountability around estimating. "Kealy, Ted, the one thing I *need* from you both is that as soon as you *think* you are going to blow an estimate, speak up and tell your project manager. And Lisa, as software project manager, you can have a discussion about the task with them to ensure that they haven't changed the scope of the task since the estimate was created. If, in fact, the estimate will be missed, you must then call the client and ask them what they want to do."

Finally, I turned to our client. "Jen, here's what you get out of all this. More aggressive estimates, more work in less time since the estimating environment is a trusting one, and dedicated team members who enjoy striving to meet their own estimates. However, you must be willing to accept that every once in a while, we'll make a mistake. And when we do, we'll inform you before we've spent all the money."

Teaching the process is a powerful empowerment tool!

The Fallacy
of Status

Udi Dahan
Haifa, Israel

AFTER A SUCCESSFUL FIRST PROJECT, I confidently embarked on my second. This was a larger project, it was more strategic to my employer, and I would manage a multidisciplinary team of people. I was sure that the skills that had served me the first time around wouldn't fail. Interestingly enough, it was my trust in my team's status reports that was my eventual undoing.

About two months into the project, my infrastructure team lead confessed, "It turns out some of the architectural assumptions we made were unfounded." However, he assured me that, "We'll be back on track by the end of the month." Despite his reassurances and the contingency buffers I had in place, I couldn't dismiss the sense that something was wrong.

At the end of the month, I followed up with the same team lead. He showed me how the refactoring work had been completed on schedule and how the developers were all set to hit their targets for the coming month. When I sat down with my integration team lead, she notified me that everything looked good from her vantage point, too. Modules were complying with their specifications, each had been sufficiently tested, and all the multiple layers of the architecture tested stable enough for the first integration.

After a slightly bumpy first integration (as many of them are) and a regular quality assurance cycle, I was astounded to discover that almost every use case had critical bugs in it. We were almost 5 months into the 15-month schedule, but nowhere near a third done with our project work.

I remained certain that all the team members would pull together to finish on time. One month before we were supposed to be going live, everyone was reporting that their work was at least 95% done. However, when I brought in one of our real users to try the system out, she told me in no uncertain terms, "This is broken in so many ways, I couldn't stand working with anything like it." That didn't sound like a project 95% done to me.

An experienced project manager, Patrick, was brought in to "save the day." While Patrick, the project savior, (and today, my mentor) was getting things back on track, he explained to me the fallacy of status. The customer defines "done," not a status report.

The fact that the database team reported 95% completion had no real bearing on whether our users could use what we developed. Even if the status reports looked perfect, they were giving an incorrect view of the project progress. In short, the project was doomed, practically from day one, because I wasn't mapping to the goals of the project.

I finally understood why I always needed to work with users to have them evaluate each feature as it was created, to be sure it added customer-perceived value. That way, the project status reports, converted to earned-value reports, show the true percentage of earned value created rather than only showing how much work is left.

What Do They Want to Hear, Anyway?

Martha Legare, MBA, PMP
Atlanta, Georgia, U.S.

PROJECT COMMUNICATION TAKES MANY FORMS—from "management by walking around" to formal presentations. I consider communication the most critical set of activities in a project.

The hardest, yet the most common, way to convey software project information from one person to the next is a formal presentation. Some polls find that public speaking is more frightening than death or the dentist!

Most presentations are too long, boring, and riddled with too much detail. Look at your last presentation and see if it could accurately be described as "death by PowerPoint®."

If your answer is "yes," you can redesign your next one so it truly communicates to your audience. Ask yourself, "What is the best mode of presentation for what I want to accomplish?" If you have a small group and want give-and-take discussions, using a flip chart or a whiteboard to capture areas of concern or agreement is a useful technique.

However, if you want executives to approve a particular project or agree to a new project tact, a multimedia slideshow could work. The trick is to realize that regardless of the technology you employ, *you* are what sells the idea to your audience—not your slides, posters, or laser light shows.

We must engage both left-brain logic and right-brain creativity in order to effectively sell our ideas. Use the statistical proof, but showcase it in a memorable format. Use easy-to-understand color charts and graphs, and just a few bullet points.

Explain the story behind each bullet point, rather than using too much text and reading it aloud a beat after participants have already read it for themselves.

Plan your presentation ahead of time using a whiteboard and sticky notes rather than starting directly with PowerPoint. Brainstorming on sticky notes allows you to see the big picture and easily rearrange ideas without feeling you are destroying hours of work.

Place your sticky notes in "affinity" groups, combining similar concepts, and then think about how to craft those ideas into a meaningful and memorable story. Always come back to the questions "What's my central point?" and "Why does it matter to this specific audience?"

Capture interest by creating curiosity or showing the unexpected, then use concrete illustrations to support your numbers with something your audience can visualize. For example, a *Wall Street Journal* article described an executive who lost enough of his company's money that if you took crisp $100 bills and stacked them on top of one another, they would reach the 92nd floor of his Madison Avenue office. That's a memorable image.

When in doubt, delete all but the essentials. You can prepare a handout for people to read later if they want more detailed information, and a take-away document will ensure that your facts won't get distorted. This approach will guarantee that you will present your essentials succinctly. And when you find out that the president has cut your presentation from 30 minutes to 5 in order to make his golf tee-time, you'll be prepared to summarize on the spot.

Recognize the Value of Team Morale

David Bock
Reston, Virginia, U.S.

MORALE IS ONE OF THOSE THINGS YOU KNOW YOU NEED, but it is hard to grow and measure. A team with high morale will occasionally put in extra effort cheerfully, but a team with low morale will not. High morale isn't just about a better workplace, it is about a more productive team.

A few years ago, I worked with a team that exhibited high morale. At times, the office felt more like a community of friends than a workplace. Productivity was high. We would occasionally have crises that required a little extra "push," and team members would volunteer for that extra effort.

A few years later, I saw that same team at an ice cream social at the office, and it didn't appear happy. The team members weren't socializing, and their body language seemed cold. When I approached them, they were complaining that there were only "chocolate Jimmies, not colored sprinkles" as a topping for the ice cream. Think about that transition: same team, same project, much different morale. It went from cheerfully working overtime, when needed, to complaining about free ice cream.

How did this happen? The team had a new manager who made some bad decisions. His errors led the team down a false path and created more work for it. Senior management blamed the entire team. And when the manager took no responsibility, the team lost confidence. The project became "more work and less fun," and morale suffered.

As the manager tried to improve the situation, he made things worse. He remembered that when the team members had high morale, they would occasionally go out to movies together. So, he instituted a "movie night." The team had no interest in socializing, and attendance was low. The manager began marking on performance reviews that people weren't "participating with the team." That lowered morale even more.

In this situation, the manager had the cause and effect backward. People don't have high team morale because they socialize; they are more willing to socialize because they have high morale.

As a consultant, I have tried to think about ways to measure morale. I have joked about metrics like "the ratio of cars in the parking lot at 5:05 p.m. and 4:55 p.m.," and the "number of visible *Dilbert* cartoons per square foot of office space." But I have realized morale isn't something to be measured, morale *is* the measurement. We are measuring the team's attitude. Morale is the measure of the team's confidence in its leader, confidence in its teammates, and faith in its own ability to get things done.

It is your job as the software project manager to create a workplace with high morale. If team members respect you as their leader, and if they feel they can talk to you and influence the outcome of events, morale will improve.

High morale results in greater satisfaction among your employees, lower turnover, and higher productivity. On top of all that, it's just nicer to be around happy people. Don't you agree?

Engage Stakeholders All Through Project Life

Lukeman Lawal, M.ENG, MNSE, R.ENGR.
Lekki, Lagos, Nigeria

GOOD WORKING RELATIONSHIPS with stakeholders who have significant influence on the outcomes of a project are vital. Stakeholders are individuals and groups, both inside and outside the organization, who can influence the success of the project, and/or anyone who can be affected by the project.

Project managers should have a stakeholder engagement plan that includes identification of stakeholders, an assessment of their degree of influence, and an assessment of their favorability toward the project. Use this plan to deliberately build support.

Engage stockholders early and keep them involved through project completion. Be sure you know the business need for the project they support. Work toward aligning the needs of all of the key stakeholders, not just the top few.

It's always pertinent to find out what the key stakeholders need to become visible and vocal advocates for the project, and how the project can be made to be a win for them, as well as for your team.

Once your project plan reflects the needs of the key stakeholders, insist that they demonstrate their commitment by providing the resources needed to support the project. This gives you an army of investors to fight outside stakeholders with no money or services who may want to stop the project.

It is advisable to assign a single point of accountability on the project team for coordinating stakeholder management, and to interface with and actively engage key stakeholders at appropriate levels. Create and utilize a stakeholder communication plan to capture frequency of communications, content of communication, and type of delivery method. Methods and frequency of contact may differ for each stakeholder.

Schedule an alignment meeting with smaller stakeholders to minimize conflicts between departments. Your stakeholder handler will follow up to ensure that critical functions/groups are represented on the core project team, or on the extended project team, as resources.

Review stakeholder standards of success with decision makers at each meeting to ensure that alignment remains consistent.

Here are some other suggestions:

- Respect the business needs of stakeholders, even if you don't agree.
- Ensure confidentiality on sensitive issues to build trust.
- Create an alliance of stakeholders to support your project.
- Get stakeholders actively and meaningfully involved.
- Solicit stakeholder ideas and use their input.
- Keep stakeholders informed.
- Leverage those with positive attitudes and get them invested—visibly if possible.

However, expect setbacks and roadblocks and be ready to address them as they occur. There will always be bumps on the road, so do not put the pressure on yourself or the stakeholders to be perfect. Just deal with these issues as they arise, and learn the lessons they will teach you so you do not have to face them again.

Engaging stakeholders early enough and keeping them involved as partners until the end of project will help you to avoid show stoppers. They may not understand the details of project management, but if you help them meet their business goals, they will join you in celebrating excellent project performance.

The Value of Planning

Derry Simmel, PMP, MBA, FLMI
Chapin, South Carolina, U.S.

"In preparing for battle I have always found that plans are useless, but planning is indispensable."
—Dwight D. Eisenhower, 34th President of the United States

SOME PROJECT MANAGERS prefer the quote, "No plan survives contact with the enemy," by General George S. Patton. They reason that it is a waste of time to create plans, since they will be invalid almost from the beginning. This attitude has doomed many projects to failure. There will always be managers who advocate action over planning. Action is seductive, planning is boring.

Boring as it may be, the sole purpose of planning is not to create a set of documents. Eisenhower realized that the discipline of planning causes you to think about your project. The planning sessions create a deeper understanding of the project. You address work, budget, resources, risks, timelines, and more. As you plan, you gain greater insight into what is needed for success. Your plans will also help you understand if, and how, goals can be achieved. Completed plans are an invaluable way to communicate about the project.

Planning documents record what was discussed and decided. They do not exist to inflexibly dictate a course of action. Unfortunately, the originals will quickly lose their value and relevance. That is why we have two types of planning: initial and ongoing.

The goal of initial planning is to set the course of the project. Initial planning looks at the project as a whole and considers all areas (risk, time, quality, etc.). The initial plan sets the intent of the project, and maps a reasonable course to the objectives. The course will change as more information is gained and the situation changes. This is natural. A change in the objectives is less common, and should only be done with caution.

To create an initial plan, you must think about your project, understand the risks and limitations, and build a path to success. As the project manager, you take your team through planning sessions to do this. Creating an initial level of mutual understanding is vital, particularly right after "first contact with the enemy…" reality.

First contact is when the act of planning pays off. Because everyone understands the plan, each member can react independently in accordance with the intent of the plan. Knowing the overall goals and restrictions allows your team to make the right decisions quickly. This is when ongoing planning kicks in.

Your ongoing planning process starts with the existing plan and modifies it to account for the new reality. You planned to start development on May 1st, but now you can't start until June 1st. How do you make up the time? Can you assign your resources to other tasks that can be done in May? Do you need more time, more money? These are your ongoing planning considerations. You plan, adjust, and then execute.

Each time you plan, you are thinking and communicating about your project. These necessary and fundamental activities will never fail to yield benefits well beyond their cost.

Don't Always Be "The Messenger"

Matt Secoske
Omaha, Nebraska, U.S.

ONE OF THE MOST IMPORTANT ROLES of the software project manager is to facilitate an open dialogue between the various members of the team. Unfortunately, I have been on many projects where the opposite has happened. The PM became the bottleneck through which all communication flowed. He or she was "The Messenger," passing precious bits of information from one team member to the next.

For a project to be organic as it progresses, information becomes the air and water feeding the code base as it grows toward fulfilling the ultimate mission of the project. All team members rely on a constant exchange of information. But if the stakeholders are forced to channel all knowledge through the PM, insurmountable problems are guaranteed.

The PM, after being entrusted with current updates, may not have correctly identified all of the developers who need to receive that information. The originator of the message thinks he/she has fulfilled any obligation by passing it along to the PM. Once the communication channel oversight is discovered, the first team member may not remember exactly what she passed along earlier, as she has since moved on to newer challenges. The PM, overwhelmed with technological reports he or she may not understand, quickly becomes incapable of being the single point of conductivity for project wisdom.

There is an even more damaging role than The Messenger, in which a well-meaning but clueless PM becomes "The Scrambler." As a project grows, so does the amount of nontechnical information needed to keep it running smoothly.

Developers need to know the business rules, the business champion needs to know the status of the deliverables, and various other people need insight into where the project stands in relation to its schedule, cost, and quality metrics.

As this amount of information grows, so does the likelihood that a non-omnipotent PM will miscommunicate. The Scrambler has struck! For example, a business rule that appears to have little impact on the project on the surface may in fact be a major roadblock once its true intent is discovered. Sizable changes to the code base may need to be done in order to repair the damages.

A project manager needs to get the right stakeholders together to talk about the right topic at the right time. Finding a time to have people from disparate departments available to meet may seem daunting. The practice? The PM, trying to solve a scheduling issue says, "Cheri, I'll take this directly to Bob, and get back to you with the answer." This can work for short, nontechnical questions. But, be aware that success in small ventures can insidiously evolve you into a Messenger or a Scrambler. Invariably something is missed in the translation, leading to excessive wasted time spent trying to sort out the repercussions.

Providing clear, open channels for communication, along with archiving discussions and decisions, allows all team members to interact directly with one another. This keeps The Messenger and The Scrambler project manager at bay, and keeps the software project moving forward.

Effectively Manage the Deliverables

Ernani Marques da Silva, MBA, PMP, PgMP
Mairipora, Sao Paulo, Brazil

PROJECTS ARE COMPRISED OF A SET OF DELIVERABLES that, when completed, constitute the completion of the whole product, service, or result. For software development projects, integrating all of the components is crucial for the final result to work properly. The components, of course, vary depending on the kind of software you are building. So, the deliverables are the major components that should actively be planned, controlled, monitored, and managed by following these tips:

- **Identify the deliverables.** Identified deliverables outline the full solution, identify the order in which they should be created and delivered, identify metrics that should be used to monitor and control their development and delivery, and actively monitor their progress against the planned baseline and metrics defined.

  It is very important to break deliverables into partial packets of code, each created to provide a special software function. This is especially important for complex projects/environments and projects developed by third parties. Do not wait to receive the full work package at the end. It is a good practice to arrange for the delivery of project parts bit by bit, and follow a preplanned process to deploy them to other members of the software team for use in their own development work.

- **Monitor and control the deliverables.** Once you have defined the means by which the work packages (functional code bits) will be built, monitored, and controlled, you must actively monitor and control the building phase to check whether the work is being done as planned. Checkpoints, metrics, and key performance indicators (KPIs) should be shared with all project team members.

At the checkpoints, the KPIs and metrics should be evaluated against the baseline and trend analysis in order to identify variances. This way, corrective action can be done based on actual metrics, rather than hunches or hearsay.

- **Manage the deliverables.** Once the anticipated work is delivered, the code should be tested and deployed to a small group of users in order to verify that it complies with requirements before it can be considered finished. This approach helps identify problems so that corrective action can be taken before the software is deployed to the entire user group.

Throughout this approach, it is very important to remember that all mini-deliverables will be ready in phases and they should be tested in an integrated fashion (like a wave). If you wait until the full code set is delivered, you could receive a body of code with a lot of unknown errors/defects or unexpected behavior. Because the product/service/result was built with these issues, their effect is both buried and multiplied. The cost and the time spent in order to fix all nonworking code at this point can be very high.

You can balance and examine the vendor's experience in your company's environment, and in the system, against the complexity required by development and decide whether this approach should be good for you or not. In general, it is most useful for complex solutions or for new technology/new solutions.

We Are Project Managers, Not Superheroes

Angyne J. Schock-Smith, PMP
Phillipsburg, New Jersey, U.S.

THIS IS A TIP THAT IS USEFUL if you're a software project manager in information technology environments, but is also transferrable to whatever type of projects you manage.

"We are project managers, not superheroes," is part of my introductory routine when I deliver training on project management skills. When talking about the characteristics of a good project manager, my favorite line is, "Get out your capes, people! It takes a superhero to do all a software project manager must do, and to do it well." However, since this comes early in the training, I have to offer some hope. So I say, "OK, some of us mere mortals actually become good project managers. What's the trick?"

I believe this trick has three parts:

- Know your personal strengths and weaknesses.

- Know the personal strengths and weaknesses of your team.

- Use this knowledge to create complementary partnerships with team members who possess strengths where you have gaps.

How can you get to know your personal strengths and weaknesses?

- Get out your copies of all the old personality or work behavior tests you've ever taken.

- Be honest as you extrapolate data from these old evaluations. Were you honest when you took the questionnaire? Does the "label" still fit, or have you grown and changed since that time? Which of the label's associated strengths and weaknesses most accurately describe you right now?

- Don't try to figure out which label would make the best project manager. There is no right answer to that question. A good project manager has to be flexible, i.e., be able to diagnose each situation and shift out of his/her comfort zone to respond in the most effective way.

- From your available data, create a fresh, current personal inventory of strengths and weaknesses. Keep it where you will always be able to find it and update it as you continue to learn more about yourself.

After that, the rest is downhill! Use an available strengths inventory to assess your team. Then, look for people on the team who have strengths in the areas listed on your personal weakness inventory.

For me (an Expressive type , if you know the Social Styles types), my weakness is attention to detail. I'll always need someone (an Analytical type) to keep me on track in that area! If you're likely to try to please others more than you should, you may need someone to help you drive the project forward more forcefully than you would be comfortable doing yourself.

Make sure that you have teammates with complementary skills working with you in areas where your weaknesses lie. But you don't have to tell them that's what you are doing, right? Keep some mystique about it, and maybe you can convince the team that you are a superhero. I won't tell anyone otherwise.

Increase Communication: Hold Frequent, Instant Meetings

Richard Sheridan
Ann Arbor, Michigan, U.S.

SOFTWARE PROJECT MANAGERS often fall into the deadly trap of regularly scheduling their teams for painful meetings that have the unfortunate, unintended effect of actually decreasing communications. One of the all-time dreaded meetings is the classic Monday morning status meeting. As if Mondays weren't bad enough already!

If you aren't convinced that most meetings should be killed, try this experiment. As the software project manager, don't show up. Ask one of your trusted colleagues about the meeting you skipped. Did they hold it without you?

If the meeting only happens when the boss or project manager shows up, kill it. Your team is telling you they don't get value out of it. Never hold meetings where only one person gets value.

At my organization, we do everything we can to eliminate unproductive meetings and replace them with simpler communication paths among team members. For example, we have the team work all day, every day, in one big open room with no walls, offices, cubes, or doors. Thus, when I need an answer from someone, I can simply say, "Hey, James." In less than 30 seconds, James and I have exchanged the necessary information and can get back to work without actually moving (or sending emails back and forth).

Imagine an all-company meeting with 60 people that is as easy to set up as shouting out "Hey, everybody!" Everyone stops what they are doing and responds, "Hey, Rich!" The meeting can take a few, short minutes and then everyone turns back to work without moving from his/her seat.

Our rituals and ceremonies include weekly "Show and Tells" to demonstrate progress on projects to sponsors, weekly "planning games" to authorize project scope, daily stand-up meetings, and weekly kick-off meetings to brainstorm about how we will work together toward common goals on client projects in the upcoming week. The meeting has a structure that makes participation easy and fun.

Try a daily stand-up meeting for one week and see if it catches on. Here are some lessons we've learned to make this meeting more effective:

- Invite everyone involved in the project. We often have 50–60 people in this meeting.

- Call the meeting with an alarm clock loud enough for everyone to hear. An impartial device calling the meeting is more likely to get participation. We use a dartboard that has an alarm clock in it.

- Use a speaking token. We use a plastic Viking helmet to control the meeting. Just hand it around the circle of people *standing* (no sitting allowed). The person who has the token has the floor.

- Have people report what they recently completed, what they are working on, and where they need help. Help doesn't come during the meeting, but afterward.

Our typical stand-up meeting takes 13 minutes! Call it, assemble it, hold it, give everyone a chance to talk, finish it, and get back to work in 13 minutes. I defy most organizations to complete a useful meeting of 60 people in 13 minutes.

Flexibility Simplifies Project Management

Krishna Kadali, M. Tech
Kondapur, Hyderabad, India

MIYAMOTO MUSASHI, A FAMOUS 17TH-CENTURY SAMURAI, believed in the principle, "Do not develop an attachment to any one weapon or any one school of fighting." This advice also rings true in our project life. It is imperative that we not get too attached to any one management principle, software tool, or programming language as our only weapon. It is only through seeing our resources in a flexible way, arrangeable in many varying configurations, that we are able to prepare the best response to the customer problems that become our project.

Take an open-minded approach right from the beginning when you define your project requirements. If you already have your weapon and fight plan chosen before you talk to the customer, how can you be sure your solution is the best one?

Before picking your weapon, examine all your customer's requirements. What problem is the customer trying to solve using your new software? The problems are usually attached to some business logic showing that the current resources aren't feature- or function-rich enough. Next, consider the pool of existing factors and systems within your organization. Reusing parts of existing environmental systems skillfully can shorten and ease your project path.

Available enterprise environment factors include such diverse things as the company infrastructure of existing facilities, equipment and software, commercial and private databases, programming tools, and human resource skills.

A resource-oriented analysis of the customer requirements to be met by the software or other project deliverables will reveal some of these underlying resources that already exist in the organization: "Our users must be able to see the XPP34 call center system side by side with our corporate accounts receivable system. Your product will need to be merged, or be compatible, with our 4465IL legacy software."

Your job is to ask the right questions about various final performance results expected by the customer, and about how existing resources/software/systems and your new code ouput are to interrelate. You may be able to lay a foundation for changes your customer will want in the future using this resource-oriented approach. At the end of this analysis, your software begins to take shape as a set of new resources—things that not only solve today's problems, but that can be used to complete future projects and interact with future software.

Once you know what the customer wants and what resources are already available within your organization, *now* you can choose your best weapon to fight the problem. Actual development can first focus on a few key requirements you deliver to gain the customer's confidence. The modules and services needed for satisfying the key requirements should be implemented first.

Leaving your mind open to new paths for software design provides a pleasant way to handle software projects in the world of constantly changing requirements. This flexibility will simplify your project management challenges, and creating fresh weapons and plans keeps your workday interesting and enriching.

The Web Points
the Way, for Now

David Wood
Fredericksburg, Virginia, U.S.

THERE IS A CHARITY GROUP WHOSE SLOGAN IS "We stand on the shoulders of those who came before us. We provide the shoulders for those who follow us." This quote is relevant for us as software developers. As each new architecture, language, or platform rises to prominence, we tend to sigh, "This is the answer to all of our programming problems." And while it may solve today's issues, tomorrow there will be new challenges facing us.

Currently, we know of exactly one software architecture that scales to billions of users and does so while being robust* to failures of individual components: the World Wide Web. The Web is the largest, most used, and most robust information retrieval system ever built by humankind—so far.

Why does the Web work so well? Roy Fielding, a founder of the vaunted Apache project,† researched this very question. Fielding evaluated the architecture of an idealized version of the early Web and extracted architectural style elements from it.

The result was a new software architectural style with the properties that we have come to love about the Web. They are robust to both change and failure of specific components. They separate concerns so we stop caring about implementation details such as programming languages. They use a common *lingua franca* (a language for communication among those who don't speak the same mother tongue) to exchange language-neutral requests for information. They scale mightily. They are stateless.

---

* *Robust*: Capable of coping well with variations, sometimes unpredictable ones, with minimal damage, alteration or loss of functionality.

† *Apache project*: An open source project to develop and maintain free web server software for modern operating systems.

Not every website uses these guiding principles, but many do, and the Web as a whole uses them. However, these are only the shoulders on which the continuous development of new and innovative architectures will rest.

We can learn important things from the Web's success. Perhaps the most important is that Moore's Law‡ now allows us to accept a great deal of abstraction in our system design. Instead of being overly efficient with our hardware and software, we can now think about being overly stable, overly robust, overly scalable, and overly flexible. And we can accept the inefficiencies of our current architectures, knowing full well that they are only a foundation for future innovations.

Distributed systems, like the Web, are hard to design. Perhaps this is because each of us is an individual. We treat our software systems like something that an individual creates, centralized as we each see the world. The Web's distributed systems have shown us the way, though. Distributed systems are harder to conceptualize, and thus harder to create, but creating them is worth the effort.

Naturally, technology changes. Ideas and techniques change, too. The simple Web of Fielding's description is not the modern Web. Nor will it be the Web of the future. The Web may not always point the way. The key to adapting to new systems will be to design flexibility into our systems now. Only then can we begin to create living, breathing, adaptive software systems that are ready to integrate with new discoveries, providing the shoulders for those who follow us.

‡ *Moore's Law*: This law describes a long-term trend in computer hardware in which the number of transistors that can be placed, inexpensively, on an integrated circuit has increased exponentially.

Developers Hate Status Reports, Managers Love Them

Pavel Simsa, PMP
Bellevue, Washington, U.S.

WORKING IN THE BIGGEST SOFTWARE COMPANY IN THE WORLD, I can attest that developers hate status reports. It makes them spend hours each week writing down what seems to them to be obvious, redundant information.

For you as a software project manager, however, this is data used to get a bigger picture of your project progress, and then passed on to upper management. On average, a project manager helms five to seven projects at a time. Both you and your senior management team need you to collect and pass on this project data.

Here are tips to make developers less resistant to sending their "whatever-frequency-you-need" status reports:

- Help them understand why this report is important to other team members or other departments that need to plan based on team progress. People work harder to help their peers.

- If the project progress was slow, know what the team was doing. Was it learning a new tool or language? Were there unexpected problems and challenges this week? When you compile the status reports, add the explanatory information to help others interpret the numbers.

- Give proper recognition. If you know what the problems and challenges were, you'll be able to make sure that no significant achievement is masked by the progress report metrics. For those who have made helpful, unplanned contributions, offer a latte coupon to a nearby coffee shop. Try a "Great work, thank you <name>" email that goes to the entire division. Create a direct link between the work and the importance of how it relates to the "big picture."

- If you're managing more than one developer, create a group incentive. "If I get all status report by 3 p.m. every Friday from all of you for one month, everyone gets the next Friday afternoon off," or, "I'll bring in food for a group lunch." Nobody wants to be the one who keeps his or her team from the reward.

- Make it easy to write the report. Provide a template or an electronic tool to submit the status. Be prepared to rewrite the verbiage in a way that will be understandable to everyone. Your vice-president most likely won't understand "lcl check-in to main build lab." You can change it to "feature milestone 2 achieved; project on track."

The point is, make sure you look at the task of completing periodic status reports from the other person's perspective. Status reports are important. Everyone needs to know what's going on. Senior management cares about milestones, while business management cares about budget. Your job as a project manager is to make sure that every stakeholder understands what's going on with the project—but also to realize that not all stakeholders are able to fully analyze all the technical nuances of what is transpiring without your help.

Find an effective input tool and work to achieve as much understanding of the underlying tasks as you can. You are the liaison to create a comprehensive status report that meets the needs of all stakeholders.

You Are Not
in Control

Patrick Kua
London, UK

I REMEMBER ONE PROJECT TEAM I COACHED. The project manager obviously had a desire to be the central point of control. He had what appeared to be an almost obsessive need to be involved in all "critical" decision-making discussions. He would actively direct the daily stand-up meeting, and he alone would decide who got to talk during project retrospective rituals. The team he managed was actually well formed by the time I arrived, and I noticed with interest how the quality of discussions differed between those where the project manager was present and those where he was not.

When I talked to a few people on the team one on one, they confessed they hated all of the meetings the project manager would hold, because they just wanted them to be over. They felt like their time was being wasted, as their real opinions were not valued. They recounted times they said the things the project manager wanted to hear to get him to move on. When they had issues that needed addressing, they would go to the technical lead. He was more willing to be part of an open discussion and, therefore, was more effective at solving problems.

The lesson I learned from this team is that acting as if you control the situation is not the same thing as actually being in control. In fact, actively seeking control sometimes creates the opposite effect. An experienced, well-formed team will actively shun a person trying to take control for personal reasons, especially if that control brings little benefit to the team.

It helps for project managers to understand group dynamics and different leadership styles. Different projects and various teams will require different levels of control. Well-formed, high-performing groups will often resent excess control unless they can see how it helps them.

The control will often be seen as "meddling" and though the groups may verbally agree, their actions after leaving the meeting may not fully reflect what you intended. However, with a newly formed team, more control may provide the group with direction and establish clearer objectives for the project.

Great project managers exert just the right level of control, respecting what skills, experiences, and connections team members bring to the project at hand. They recognize the signs when more control may help move the group toward its ultimate goal, as well as recognizing the signs when the same control may be slowing the group down.

Nowhere is this more crucial than when a non-IT project manager is asked to lead a software development project. The team, often resentful of outside interference in its workspace, may devalue the skill set the project manager brings to the project.

But the organizational skills, the ability of the project manager to keep the project in line with company goals, and the successful care of communication lines between upper management and the customer can protect the IT team and leave its members free to work.

Share the Vision

Jared Richardson
Morrisville, North Carolina, U.S.

DO YOU WORK WITH IDIOTS? Do your team members want to bankrupt the company? Sometimes it feels that way, but it's usually not the case. The truth is, everyone wants to succeed and feel proud of their contributions, no matter how much it appears that they're trying to sabotage your project. They are doing what they think is the right thing, but everyone has a different idea of what "right" is.

As the software project manager, how do you get everyone working together? Know that most teams labor in darkness. They don't know why this project matters, how it fits into the company's larger strategy, or why the deadline is June 17th. Since they don't understand why certain decisions were made, the choices appear arbitrary and irrational. Everyone struggles, trying to form a clear vision of this murky situation without any definitive information to help them. Should we be surprised that everyone see a different end goal to the project?

To clear away the fog, you need to share with your team members the key pieces of data that will make them knowledgeable about your common endeavor. Let them know that the project needs to ship in mid-June to beat a competitor's product to market by three weeks. Help them understand that this project fills a need in a larger corporate strategy to expand internationally, or that your customer is counting on it to shore up dwindling profits from its existing, but aging, product line.

Be careful, if you're new at sharing information. As the conduit of information for your team, you'll also be shaping the team's morale. When you decide to gripe about another group or manager, or a member of your team, your negative attitude can spread through your team as quickly as the flu. And, like a viral infection, it can slow your team's verve for days.

A great way to share project information is to hold a daily meeting. Teams with 10 people or so can meet effectively in as little as 10–20 minutes. Each person has a one- to two-minute opportunity to bring the team up-to-date on his own progress and ask for help, if he needs it. These quick "standups" are the perfect place for the software project manager to share project updates.

When you opt for a weekly (or monthly) meeting, you may forget important information; after all, it's old news to you by the time the group finally assembles. Or a problem that could have been prevented blows up because you delayed sharing risk indicators. Perhaps the team will glaze over after you've shared 17 bits of "vital" information all stuffed into one, bloated team talk.

Remember, your team, and everyone at your company, wants to succeed. Share your vision and ask others to share theirs. You'll find most of those idiots you thought were out to close the company are actually people who will work side-by-side with you to solve mutually understood team challenges.

True Success Comes with a Supporting Organization

Cynthia A. Berg, PhD (ABD), PMP
Glendale, Arizona, U.S.

IF ORGANIZATIONS AVOID RISK PLANNING, aggressive problem seeking, and timely issue resolutions, it could be due to a problem with the culture. Those on a project team who play the devil's advocate are often labeled as troublemakers. If the organization is quick to "shoot the messenger," team members will avoid sharing troublesome issues and there may be an inclination to hide project problems.

This type of cultural setting encourages blaming behaviors that work to the detriment of the entire organization, individual employees, and the customers. The role of the software project manager is to provide a predictable project delivery, with as few unexpected events as possible. With no one pointing out pitfalls early, there are often "surprises." Seldom are they good surprises, but rather, ugly ones showing that foresight and planning were impossible as developers hid issues from exposure.

Wise executives will make sure the company is supporting the attitudes and behaviors that allow developers to be effective. This includes evaluating human resource policies and incentive plans to make sure that they are aligned with behaviors that lead to the development of strong products and services.

A classic example of misalignment is an organization that officially "preaches" teamwork, but then consistently rewards individual contributions. People are smart; they know which path serves their own best interests. If upper management can establish consistency between what it professes to believe and what it provides as a work environment to encourage productive behavior, both the individuals and the organization can flourish.

For those of you who find yourselves in nonsupportive or dysfunctional organizations, here are some steps you can take:

- Ask and ask until you understand the scope of the project so you can work within it.

- Locate probable team members and other stakeholders. Whenever possible, include them in brainstorming, planning, and project execution.

- Allow the people who are doing the work to fully participate in project updates and decisions, at least until they finish their activities on this project.

- Always be an honest software project manager. Never gloss over or simplify problems to avoid conflict or uncomfortable discussions.

- Provide the environment within your project team that you'd like to see mirrored by the whole organization.

Project managers must be objective about the project. They occupy the unenviable role of owing their first allegiance to the organization that pays them, while at the same time needing to build a trust situation with the developers. If the project outlook looks bleak, an astute and principled project manager should make a recommendation that it be cancelled until peripheral problems can be addressed.

We all want to work in an organization with a cohesive strategy to support new software project development. But sadly, that capability level may vary enormously even among departments within a single organization. Since moving toward a more supportive environment benefits all, it should become a part of the software project manager's role to alert upper management to cultural conflicts between project priorities and performance rewards.

Establish Project Management Governance

Ernani Marques da Silva, MBA, PMP, PgMP
Mairipora, Sao Paulo, Brazil

A PROJECT CAN INTERACT WITH A WIDE GROUP comprised of team members, vendor team members, customers or project sponsors, operational teams, contract teams, financial teams, and other relevant stakeholders. In this scenario, where the project involves a large group of people, a variety of situational things can jeopardize the project.

If you are a software project manager coming from an information technology background, it may be helpful for you to know how to fit into the larger view of project management outside your department.

Governance is a management method that is used to develop, communicate, implement, and monitor polices, procedures, practices, and other acts used to run a project. Putting an effective project governance structure and procedure into place helps ensure the project alignment, monitoring and controlling of threats and opportunities, decision making, and delivery of project packages that are focused on the project planned. It allows you to appropriately address the risk and consequently meet the project requirements.

To be effective, the project governance should be planned in advance. Address relevant items in its framework like the governance goals and objectives; the structure; the principles; the process, procedures, and standards; communication; reporting relationships; escalation procedures (what, when, how, by whom); tools; clearly defined and applied responsibilities and accountabilities; measurements and criteria for measurements; quality; meeting and steering committees; audits; and monitoring and control.

Bear in mind that the governance can be affected by a series of factors: environmental, sector, industry, company culture, and legislation. For example, in a functional organization you, as project manager, may be directly reporting to a functional manager rather than to a portfolio or program manager. The project manager has the most power in a projectized organization, where all work is set up as projects. However, in a functional organization model, you could report directly to a line or department manager, effectively weakening your power.

So, consider the organizational hierarchy when you plan and define the governance architecture. The structure can be modified, as needed, based on the evolution and progress of the work in order to keep the project aligned with its planned goals and objectives. On a large project, align your work with larger program or portfolio objectives and goals. But create or adapt a project governance model, even if you manage a very small project.

Typically, the project management office (PMO) is responsible for defining and managing project-related procedures and processes, and creating the templates that should be followed.

The project board is an organizational body responsible for assuring that the project goals are achieved. It provides support for addressing the project risks appropriately, and for other issues as well. Some other board functions follow:

- Approving project plans and changes to the plan
- Collecting input for progress reporting
- Ensuring compliance with policies, procedures, standards, and requirements
- Providing guidance on risks and issues
- Reviewing project progress

Project governance should operate in an integrated fashion with other organization's governance structures when the project is interacting with other companies.

9.7 Reasons I Hate Your Website

Barbee Davis, MA, PHR, PMP
Omaha, Nebraska, U.S.

MOST COMPANIES DON'T KNOW that software and web development differ, so software project managers and software developers are asked to create websites. Here are 9.7 ways you can keep me from ever doing business with your company due to your annoying website:

1. **Start off with a slow-loading Flash screen.** Don't let me bypass it, then continue to make me wait endlessly as each page refreshes. The fast response times of your competitors are calling me.

2. **Surprise me with startling, ear-deafening video clips.** I may be at work, at home next to a sleeping child or spouse, or trying to buy a surprise gift. If you really want to keep me away, omit an Off button.

3. **Disable the Back button.** You feel clever by keeping me from returning to the search engine that got me to your website, but I won't be trapped twice. Next time, I won't click on your page or buy any product or service you sell.

4. **Choose a low-visibility color scheme.** Gray type on a slightly darker gray background may be unique, but it isn't readable. There are 25 other websites at a mouse click where I don't have to go blind to read information. Also, reverse type (like white on black) that doesn't allow me to easily cut and paste means I can't save your data for future purchasing decisions.

5. **Ignore my portable devices.** I may carry an iPhone, Kindle, or netbook computer. If you don't have a quick, low-overhead, mobile interface, you're not the modern organization I need. We're headed away from the client/server model, back to the old "dumb terminal" hooked to a powerful computer in the sky. Plan for it.

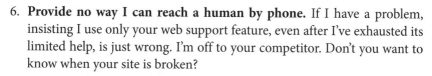

6. **Provide no way I can reach a human by phone.** If I have a problem, insisting I use only your web support feature, even after I've exhausted its limited help, is just wrong. I'm off to your competitor. Don't you want to know when your site is broken?

7. **Insist I call to get information.** Unless you are selling a never-before-created product, such as teleportation to Saturn, you know your pricing. Show it to me. Competitors can get it by calling as a phony customer. Meanwhile, you have lost me as a real one.

8. **Discriminate between customer types.** I can get an older operating system if I'm a business, so I should not be forced to upgrade to an unstable new one just because I'm an individual. If I search an airline site for a round-trip schedule, I want to see all the same flights listed if I prefer to choose multicity flights, one by one.

9. **Include a useless search function.** I want to search your website content, not just the public relations news releases regarding my search topic.

9.7 **Mislabel your buttons.** If the Read More button takes me to a video clip, I'm angry. I want to scan your text-based information, not sit through an entire presentation.

Don't make me hate you!

Contributors

Matteo Becchi, PMP (Arlington, Virginia, U.S.)

Matteo Becchi is a certified project management professional (PMP)® constantly seeking that next challenging career. He is experienced in IT application upgrades, enhancements, and implementation projects, as well as hardware-specific IT projects such as technology refreshes or data center equipment migration and consolidation projects. Matteo has experience managing direct reports as well as a diverse mix of project types and related stakeholder groups. While he has experience with SDLCs (software development life cycles) and firmly supports the Project Management Institute's (PMI) five project life cycle phases across the nine knowledge areas, he is constantly pursuing ways to improve and perfect business processes (within project management and beyond) in order to elevate the work environment to higher levels of efficiency and effectiveness.

Matteo recently completed his master's degree in information systems and technology at the George Washington University and is currently enrolled in a graduate-level Leadership Development certificate program. He is also fluent in Italian and proficient in Spanish.

Matteo can be reached at *matteo.becchi@gmail.com.*

Cynthia A. Berg, PhD (ABD), PMP (Glendale, Arizona, U.S.)

Cynthia Berg is owner of C.A. Berg and Associates, and does consulting in leadership development and project management implementation. She was with Medtronic for 20 years, most recently as principal project management specialist at Medtronic Arizona Device Manufacturing in Tempe, Arizona, where she worked with new product development projects and development of project management training and methodology. During her tenure there, she also supported organizations within Medtronic, from manufacturing to finance and new product development.

Cynthia is a senior faculty member at Keller Graduate School of Management where she teaches in the Masters of Project Management program and the MBA programs; she has been with Keller since 2000. She is also an adjunct faculty member at Rio Salado Community College, where she teaches business and project management to corporate clients and was named Outstanding Adjunct Faculty Member for the 2000–2001 academic year.

Cynthia's educational background includes a PhD in organizational behavior from Capella University, where she is currently completing her dissertation in the area of downsizing, survivor syndrome, and employee motivation; an MBA from Arizona State University; and bachelor's degrees in both psychology and sociology from The College of St. Catherine.

Cynthia has been active as a volunteer for the Project Management Institute since 1991 on both local and international levels, and earned her PMP® in 1993. Cynthia led the update of *The Guide to the Project Management Body of Knowledge* (2000 Edition), and was named PMI Linn Stuckenbrook Person of the Year 2001. She participated in the Standards MAG from 2000 through 2003, and prior to that was a member of PMI's standards committee from 1995 through 1999. She is currently project leader for the creation of a "Project Management Risk Practice Standard."

Her other interests include scuba diving (she is a PADI-certified Dive Master and Master Diver), fitness, counted cross-stitch and embroidery, and creating stained glass—as well as, of course, reading.

David Bock (Reston, Virginia, U.S.)

David Bock is a principal consultant at CodeSherpas, a company he founded in 2007. David is also the president of the Northern Virginia Java Users Group, the editor of O'Reilly's OnJava.com website, and a frequent speaker on technology in venues such as the No Fluff Just Stuff Software Symposiums.

In January 2006, David was honored by being awarded the title of Java Champion by a panel of esteemed leaders in the Java community in a program sponsored by Sun. There are approximately 100 active Java Champions worldwide.

David has also served on several JCP panels, including the specification of the Java 6 Platform and the Java Module System.

David Diaz Castillo, MBA, PMP (Panama City, Panama)

David Díaz Castillo is the project manager office director for Project Management Consultants in Panama City, Panama. He has worked in governments and private projects in different industries including IT, legal, and human resources. He is a systems engineer, and has an MBA in finance and a graduate degree in project management. He earned his PMP® in 2007.

Udi Dahan (Haifa, Israel)

Udi Dahan is an internationally renowned expert on software architecture and design. Recognized four years in a row with the coveted "Most Valuable Professional" award by Microsoft Corporation for solutions architecture and connected systems, Udi is also on the advisory board of Microsoft's next-generation technology platforms: WCF/WF/OSLO, the Software Factories Initiative, and the Composite Application Library and Guidance.

Udi is one of 33 experts in Europe recognized by the International .NET Association (INETA); an author and trainer for the International Association of Software Architects on Reliability, Availability, and Scalability; and an SOA, Web Services, and XML Guru recommended by *Dr. Dobb's*—the world's largest software magazine. When not consulting, training, and speaking, Udi leads NServiceBus—the most popular open source .NET Enterprise Service Bus.

From web projects in small Internet startups—including government projects that push the limits of technology, to enterprise-scale programs with hundreds of developers and testers costing tens of millions of dollars—companies in all verticals and of all sizes entrust Udi with providing them relevant and reliable architecture and design for their current and future requirements.

Udi can be contacted via his blog: *UdiDahan.com.*

Matt "Boom" Daniel (Coopersburg, Pennsylvania, U.S.)

Matt "Boom" Daniel is a 12-year United States Marines fighter pilot, Top-Gun graduate, and weapons officer. Boom has mentored and trained officers in the art of small-unit leadership, fighter aircraft tactics, and the competencies of operations planning, execution, and logistics. Matt facilitates business discussions among CEOs and senior executives toward the goal of real-world problem solving and strategic development. A 1985 graduate of Virginia Military Institute with a BS in civil engineering, Boom started his leadership and management consulting business, Business Battlefield, Inc., in January of 2004. Married with four boys, Boom and his family live in Coopersburg, Pennsylvania.

Barbee Davis, MA, PHR, PMP (Omaha, Nebraska, U.S.)

Barbee Davis, MA, PHR, PMP, writes a semi-monthly column for the Project Management Institute's (PMI) *Community Post*, which reaches over 400,000 project managers around the world. She is an international reviewer for training organizations wishing to be accepted or renewed into the Registered Education Program (R.E.P.) for PMI.

With a background that includes owning a computer software training company for desktop and technical application instruction and certification, it makes sense that Barbee is a Black Belt in Microsoft Project. In fact, she previously coauthored *How To Learn Microsoft Project in 24 Hours*.

Barbee has managed projects for companies all over the United States, trained hundreds of project managers for certification, taught extensively at the university level, and is sought after as a guest speaker. You may have met her at the desk on the No Fluff Just Stuff tour in the United States or Canada.

Monte Davis, MCSE (Omaha, Nebraska, U.S.)

Monte Davis has been involved with Windows server administration, information technology project management, server backup and recovery, email administration, new server rollouts, LAN/WAN administration, and second-level support since he joined MSI in March 2006. Monte's technical capabilities include all versions of Windows server administration, Cisco IOS, Linux, Lotus Domino, Microsoft Exchange 2003, and TCP/IP.

Monte was previously employed with Retalix, formerly Integrated Distributed Systems, for five years as a network administration manager and site administrator. He worked for ExecuTrain as an enterprise network administrator for five years in server administration, LAN/WAN administration, and email administration. He also taught Microsoft Official Curriculum courses.

Monte has a bachelor's degree from Northwest Missouri State University and is a member of a VMware user group.

His certifications include Microsoft Certified Systems Engineer—Microsoft Windows Server 2003; Microsoft Certified Systems Administrator—Microsoft Windows Server 2003; Microsoft Certified Systems Engineer Microsoft—Windows 2000; Microsoft Certified Systems Engineer Microsoft—Windows NT 4.0; and Microsoft Certified Professional MCP 2.0—Certified Professional.

Scott Davis (Broomfield, Colorado, U.S.)

Scott Davis published one of the first public websites implemented in Grails in 2006 and has been actively working with the technology ever since.

Author of many books, such as *Groovy Recipes: Greasing the Wheels of Java and GIS for Web Developers* (Pragmatic) and two ongoing IBM developer-Works article series (*Mastering Grails* and, in 2009, *Practically Groovy*), Scott writes extensively about how Groovy and Grails are the future of Java development.

Scott teaches public and private classes on Groovy and Grails for startups and Fortune 100 companies. He is the cofounder of the Groovy/Grails Experience conference and is a regular presenter on the international technical conference circuit (including No Fluff Just Stuff, JavaOne, OSCON, TheServerSide, and QCON).

In 2008, Scott was voted the top Rock Star at JavaOne for his talk "Groovy, the Red Pill: How to blow the mind of a buttoned-down Java developer."

You can contact Scott through his company, ThirstyHead, at *thirstyhead.com*.

Neal Ford (Atlanta, Georgia, U.S.)

Neal Ford is software architect and meme wrangler at ThoughtWorks, a global IT consultancy with an exclusive focus on end-to-end software development and delivery. He is also the designer and developer of applications, instructional materials, magazine articles, courseware, and video/DVD presentations, and he is author and/or editor of five books spanning a variety of technologies. He focuses on designing and building large-scale enterprise applications.

Neal is also an internationally acclaimed speaker, speaking at over 100 developer conferences worldwide and delivering more than 600 talks. Check out his website at *http://www.nealford.com*. He welcomes feedback and can be reached at *nford@thoughtworks.com*.

Jorge Gelabert, PMP (Berlin, Connecticut, U.S.)

Jorge Gelabert is a certified PMP® who works for Northeast Utilities as a project manager. He holds a BS in computer engineering from the University of Bridgeport in Connecticut, holds an MS in computer science from Rensselaer Polytechnic Institute (R.P.I.), speaks Spanish (native) and English, is a Delphi Document Management Professional, and holds Masters and Advanced Masters Certificates in project management from George Washington University.

Jorge is an active member of the Project Management Institute (PMI), having served as director of marketing, president, and past president of the Southern New England Chapter of PMI. Currently, he serves as the Component Mentor for Region 3, supporting 19 PMI chapters. He is also a member of the PMI-ISIG and IEEE associations.

Dr. Paul Giammalvo, CDT, CCE, MScPM (Jakarta, Indonesia)

Dr. Paul D. Giammalvo, CDT, PMP, CCE, MScPM, is senior technical advisor (Project Management) to PT Mitratata Citragraha (PTMC) in Jakarta, Indonesia (*www.getpmcertified.com*). He is also an adjunct professor of project and program management at the Lille Graduate School of Management in Paris, France (*www.esc-lille.com*). For 14+ years, he has been providing project management training and consulting throughout south and eastern Asia, the Middle East, and Europe. He is also active in the global project management community, serving as an advocate for and on behalf of the global practitioner. He does so by playing an active professional role in the Association for the Advancement of Cost Engineering International (AACE), the Construction Specifications Institute (CSI), and the Construction Management Association of America (CMAA). He also sits on the board of directors of the Global Alliance for Project Performance Standards (GAPPS; *www.globalpmstandards.org*) in Sydney, Australia, and develops graduate level curricula in asset and project management for Western Australia University, Perth (*www.blendedlearning.ecm.uwa.edu.au*).

Paul has spent 18 of the last 35 years working on large, highly technical international projects, including such prestigious projects as the Negev Airbase Project (part of the Camp David Peace Accords) in Ovda, Israel, and the Alyeska Pipeline and the Distant Early Warning Site (DEW Line) upgrades in Alaska. Most recently, he worked as a senior project cost and scheduling consultant for Caltex Minas Field in Sumatra, and project manager for the Taman Rasuna Apartment Complex for Bakrie Brothers in Jakarta. His current client list includes AT&T, Ericsson, Nokia, Lucent, General Motors, Siemens, Conoco-Philips, Unocal, BP, Dames and Moore, SNC Lavalin, Freeport McMoran, Caltex, the UN Projects Office, the World Bank Institute, and many other multinational companies and NGO organizations.

Paul holds an undergraduate degree in construction management and an MS in project management from George Washington University. He was recently awarded his PhD in project and program management through the Institute Superieur De Gestion Industrielle (ISGI) and Ecole Superieure De Commerce De Lille (ESC-Lille), under the supervision of Dr. Christophe Bredillet, CCE, IPMA A Level.

Karen Gillison (Leesburg, Virginia, U.S.)

Karen Gillison has a background in computer science and 15 years of experience developing and delivering software and systems across a broad range of industries and technologies. Karen provides software development and project management services to commercial and government clients.

Karen is a member of the RubyNation organizing committee, Northern Virginia Ruby User's Group, and Java User's Group; a Golden Spike alumna of the Pragmatic Studio Ruby on Rails; and winner of the FGM Technical Achievement Award for 2000 and 2006.

Karen lives in Virginia with her husband, Charles; their two children; and two Labrador retrievers.

James Graham, PMP (Ta' l-Ibrag, Malta)

James Graham is an independent management consultant who operates globally.

He specializes in human resource development, designing and delivering management development programs, as well as consulting in business process improvement and corporate structure.

As well as possessing a PMP® certification, James is a fellow of the Institution of Analysts and Programmers, and holds a master's degree in consulting and a diploma in psychology.

He lives on the island of Malta, in the Southern Mediterranean region of Europe.

Alan Greenblatt (Sudbury, Massachusetts, U.S.)

Alan Greenblatt brings 25 years of software development, technical management expertise, and entrepreneurship to his role as founder and CEO of Sciova, a services firm specializing in the development of enterprise semantic applications. As VP of Semantic Technologies at Metatomix, Alan spent several years playing an integral role in the development of the company's advanced semantic technology platform and holds patents associated with that work. He has worked regularly with customers such as Airbus Industries, State Street Bank, and UCB Pharma, helping them develop unique and highly valuable semantic applications in their respective organizations. Over the years Alan has contributed significantly to the development of advanced media technologies offered by both Sun Microsystems and Microsoft. He cofounded Anyware Fast, a software consultancy, and was instrumental in its sale to Dimension X, one of the very first Java startups, specializing in virtual reality and interactive multimedia–authoring software. At Dimension X, Alan was the director of technology until the firm was acquired by Microsoft. As part of the Microsoft Office team, he led the development of Microsoft Vizact 2000, an interactive multimedia authoring product.

Alan has a Bachelor of Applied Science in electrical engineering from the University of Waterloo.

Kim Heldman, PMP (Lakewood, Colorado, U.S.)

Kim Heldman, PMP, has over 18 years experience in information technology project management. She is the chief information officer for the Colorado Department of Transportation and is responsible for all IT resource planning, budgeting, and project management for a $1 billion organization with 3,300+ geographically dispersed employees.

Kim has served in an executive leadership role for several years and is regarded as a strategic visionary with an innate ability to collaborate with diverse groups and organizations, instill hope and improve morale, and lead her teams in achieving goals they never thought possible.

Kim has extensive experience in the government sector managing projects of various size and scope. She serves on the Executive Governance Committee (EGC) in the Governor's Office of Information Technology, which is responsible for oversight and governance of IT state-certified projects. In her role as cochair of the Colorado CIO Forum, Kim assisted with the recommendation and review of statewide IT policies, standards, and initiatives. Kim is also the cofounder of the Colorado Project Management Users Group, open to all state agency CIOs and IT project managers. She contributed to the development and implementation of project management policies, standards, and methodologies for projects statewide. The group's work was instrumental in helping to establish legislation requiring all major IT projects in the state of Colorado to have certified project managers conducting them.

Kim is the bestselling author of the *PMP® Project Management Professional Study Guide*, published by Sybex, Inc. and now in its fourth edition. Thousands of people worldwide have used the Study Guide for their successful preparation to sit for the PMP® exam. Kim is also the author of *Project Management JumpStart*, Second Edition, and *Project Manager's Spotlight on Risk Management* (both from Jossey-Bass). She is the coauthor of *Excel 2007 for Project Managers* and *PMP® Project Management Professional Study Guide Deluxe Edition*, Second Edition (both from Sybex).

Kim also writes on leadership topics and speaks at conferences and events. She lives in Arvada, Colorado, with her husband, Bill, and three grown children.

Naresh Jain (Malad, Mumbai, India)

Naresh Jain is a software craftsman working for Directi as a quality and community evangelist. He helps software organizations deliver quality software solutions using agile and lean thinking. He has worked on a variety of software projects utilizing XP, Scrum, and Crystal techniques since 2003.

Naresh is passionate about building a community of talented and capable software craftsmen, the next-generation software leaders in India. In recognition of his accomplishments, in 2007 the Agile Alliance awarded Naresh with the Gordon Pask Award for contributing to the Agile Community by establishing Agile User Groups in India and creating the Simple Design and Testing conference.

Naresh is the founder and vice-chairman of the Agile Software Community of India (ASCI). He has organized various conferences, including the Simple Design and Testing Conference (SDTConf) and Agile Coach Camp. Naresh has helped start various agile user groups, including the Agile Philly User Group and various groups in India.

Naresh is an active open source committer and enjoys teaching software development courses in universities. By being a part of the team, Naresh helps software companies embrace agile.

Naresh enjoys beer, music, adventure sports, and hot food of any color. You can reach him at *naresh@agilefaqs.com*.

Krishna Kadali, M. Tech (Kondapur, Hyderabad, India)

Krishna Kadali has more than 19 years of hands-on experience in technology and building businesses around technology solutions. Krishna has been part of high-technology startups, as well as publicly traded companies, where he played a key role in building successful businesses around software products. He is currently leading a systems and data integration service provider based out of Hyderabad, India, called Prabhavat Solutions, which provides several systems and data integration solutions.

Prior to founding Prabhavat, Krishna was founder and CTO at Nimaya, based in McLean, Virginia, where he spearheaded the development of its flagship products, ActionBridge and InSync, and also delivered several other customer data integration and systems integration solutions. As a part of Nimaya, he has built an offshore team in India from the ground up and successfully delivered several technology solutions through the offshore team.

Prior to founding Nimaya, Krishna served in various capacities at MKS in Fairfax, Virginia, and BULL S.A. in Paris, France, providing major contributions to architecture, design, development, and delivery of their flagship products—NuTCRACKER and OSIAPI, respectively—with extensive systems programming background.

Krishna has a master's degree in telecommunications from the Indian Institute of Technology in Kharagpur, India, and a bachelor's degree in electronics and communications from Jawaharlal Nehru Technological University in Anantapur, India.

Patrick Kua (London, UK)

Patrick Kua is an agile coach, facilitator, and developer for ThoughtWorks. He has been working with individuals on teams in agile environments for the last four years, and understands how powerful and responsive people can be when working together in a common manner. He is always interested in aspects of continuous improvement, and how lightweight processes can boost team effectiveness. He brings a blend of deep technical skills and deep understanding of management processes to teams that help them move toward their goals.

Anupam Kundu (New York, New York, U.S.)

Anupam Kundu is a project manager/lead consultant at ThoughtWorks, primarily based out of the New York area. Anupam comes from a broad consultancy background and offers specific experience for managing large-scale projects in multiple business domains, including HR/intranet systems in investment banking/private equity firms, telecom BACC in North America, global publishing and media, senior healthcare systems, and title insurance. Anupam has more than nine years of experience in various stages of requirements gathering, estimation, analysis and design, implementation, quality control, training, and post-implementation activities for software projects with premier enterprises.

Lukeman Lawal, M.ENG, MNSE, R.ENGR. (Lekki, Lagos, Nigeria)

Lukeman Lawal is a project engineer with Chevron Nigeria Limited. He manages oil and gas projects—engineering designs, construction, and installation. Lukeman was a project engineer on Escravos Gas Project Phase 3A (EGP3A) Offshore, New Oil Fields development. He presently works as an early concept development project engineer.

Lukeman was an academic staff member at the Department of Mechanical Engineering,University of Benin, Benin City, Nigeria.

Martha Legare, MBA, PMP (Atlanta, Georgia, U.S.)

Martha Legare has been a coach, trainer, and consultant in North America and Europe for almost 20 years. She is CEO of the Gantt Group, a consulting and training firm linking strategic planning, project management, and behavioral science. While the Gantt Group has a variety of clients, it focuses on the marketing and advertising industry.

Martha has designed and delivered numerous seminars, including Loyola University's Project Management Certificate for its MBA program, where she is adjunct faculty. She is published in the AMA Trainers' Activity Book. Martha has written project methodologies and helped develop project offices in the U.S., Mexico, and Europe.

Martha is a certified PMP® and certified mediator for the American Arbitration Association. She received her MBA from Almeda University and her BA from Guilford College. She is an innately strategic thinker with strong cross-cultural skills and a steadfast commitment to improving clients' businesses.

James Leigh (Toronto, Ontario, Canada)

James Leigh is an independent software consultant based in Toronto, and has been building web solutions for 10 years. He is experienced with modelling business problems and concepts in software, and specializes in performance and technology integration. His background is in semantic web technologies and decentralized networks.

James has also led semantic-related open source software projects, including Sesame's federated RDF store, relation RDF store, server client library for Sesame, integration of Mulgara and Sesame, and the object RDF mapper of OpenRDF. He has also led optimization efforts for various Java applications for over five years, including benchmarking and optimizing Sesame's RDF stores, AMC theatres' employee scheduling system, and a manufacturing tracking system for swimwear designers Christina and Gottex.

Craig Letavec, PMP, PgMP, MSP (Waynesville, Ohio, U.S.)

Craig Letavec has served as a project, program, and enterprise PMO manager in a diverse range of companies including Procter & Gamble, Hewlett-Packard, and Siemens AG. His experience includes leading global software development and implementation projects, developing and implementing project and program management offices, and developing and presenting project management training courses. Craig holds the Project Management Professional (PMP)®, Program Management Professional (PgMP)®, and Managing Successful Programmes (MSP) certifications as well as an MS in project management from George Washington University. He is the author of *The Program Management Office: Establishing, Managing, and Growing the Value of a PMO*, a bestselling reference book on the topics of PMO development and management, and *Program Management Professional (PgMP)®: A Certification Study Guide with Best Practices for Maximizing Business Results* (both from J. Ross Publishing).

Randy Loomis, PMP (Andover, Connecticut, U.S.)

Randy Loomis is a certified PMP® with over 14 years of project management experience, and has worked in the information technology field for 26 years. He is currently employed by Northeast Utilities as a project manager in the IT Program Management Office. Randy graduated cum laude from Eastern Connecticut State University with a degree in psychology.

Kim MacCormack (Leesburg, Virginia, U.S.)

Kim MacCormack is a cofounder of CodeSherpas, Inc., a software consultancy that brings her software engineering experience to commercial and government clients. In this role, she's committed to developing high-quality web applications, helping her clients get their products to market faster.

Kim has more than 13 years of software and systems engineering experience. She has designed and developed a variety of web-based and client server applications. She received her master's degree in software engineering in 2005. Kim was also an early adopter of Ruby on Rails and is a Golden Spike alumna of the Pragmatic Studio Ruby on Rails Training Course. In addition, she is a member of the Northern Virginia Java Users Group and Ruby Users Group.

Kim has experience with every aspect of the software engineering life cycle, including requirements analysis, design, human/computer interface (HCI) design, code development, and verification/validation. She has served as a project manager, technical lead, and/or software engineer for over 30 web applications for various commercial, nonprofit, and government clients. These projects included basic websites, intranets, e-commerce applications, content management systems, and complex web-based survey tools to create customized surveys with full multilingual support.

Kathy MacDougall (Erie, Colorado, U.S.)

Kathy MacDougall is chief business architect at Zepheira, which provides solutions to effectively integrate, navigate, and manage data across personal, group, and enterprise boundaries. As chief business architect, Kathy is responsible for analyzing clients' current business architecture and making recommendations for improvements to ensure successful adoption of new technology implementations.

Kathy has extensive experience leading enterprise-wide initiatives to help companies evaluate, manage, and leverage their corporate data to increase revenues and uncover new business intelligence. Successes during her 20-year tenure in this field include creating data-based and knowledge management solutions for companies ranging from $500 million to $11 billion in size, including such names as General Electric and Sun Microsystems.

Since 2000, Kathy has been implementing solutions using semantic web technologies. At Sun Microsystems, Kathy and her team led the first known large-scale corporate implementation of semantic web technologies, which provides the foundation for dynamic delivery of content from across the organization. With the proper combination of technology and business infrastructure in place, Sun was able to achieve an estimated cost avoidance of $10M annually. Kathy and team were invited to provide their expert perspective on the role of semantic web technologies in business solutions at W3C's Technical Plenary in 2003.

Kathy is a graduate of Colgate University and has extensive training in processes improvement and effecting organizational change, including background in Six Sigma methodologies.

Ernani Marques da Silva, MBA, PMP, PgMP (Mairipora, Sao Paulo, Brazil)

Ernani Marques has over 19 years of broad-based and successful experience in project management, program management, and portfolio management within the IT, banking, and services industries. He has led and managed project/program management offices (PMOs), as well as multiple projects and teams.

His experience within the IT industry includes managing projects and programs in the areas of application development, product management, and system integration utilizing full System Development Life Cycle (SDLC) processes and project management methodologies.

Alex Miller (Ballwin, Missouri, U.S.)

Alex Miller is a tech lead and engineer at Terracotta, Inc., the makers of the open source Java clustering product Terracotta. Prior to Terracotta, Alex worked at BEA Systems on the AquaLogic product line and was chief architect at MetaMatrix. His interests include Java, concurrency, distributed systems, query languages, and software design.

Alex enjoys writing his blog at *http://tech.puredanger.com*. He is a contributing author to the 2008 release *The Definitive Guide to Terracotta* (Apress), along with the rest of the Terracotta team. Alex is a frequent speaker at Java user group meetings, the No Fluff Just Stuff tour, and conferences like JavaOne.

William J. Mills (Castro Valley, California, U.S.)

William J. Mills is currently a Technical Yahoo! working primarily on software and product security at Yahoo!. Prior to that, he worked at Invisible Worlds (now defunct); at Wells Fargo, running firewalls and working on its first Internet banking release; at various contracting gigs; and for a while at the County of San Diego Superior Court.

Gennady Mironov, CPM (Toronto, Ontario, Canada)

Gennady Mironov was born in 1967. He served two years in the Soviet Army and graduated from Power Engineering Technical University in Moscow in 1992 with a master's degree in electrical engineering. He received his post-grad education in psychology and business in 2001.

Gennady has been working for last 16 years in the IT/telecommunications industry in roles from field technician to solutions manager to program manager. In the last four years before he immigrated to Canada, he managed huge wireless projects across Russia, based on Siemens and Huawei solutions. He was directly responsible for projects up to $16 million USD.

In 2008, Gennady finished a one-year post-grad program at Humber Institute of Applied Technology in project management in Toronto. He recently applied at PMI for his PMP® exam.

He lives in Toronto with his wife and three children.

Jared Richardson (Morrisville, North Carolina, U.S.)

Jared Richardson is the coauthor of the book *Ship It! A Guide to Successful Software Projects* (Pragmatic), which is now available in five languages. He works with NFJS One to help teams and managers who want an external point of view. Jared can be found on the Web at *http://AgileArtisans.com* and *http://NFJSOne.com*.

Brian Sam-Bodden (Scottsdale, Arizona, U.S.)

Brian Sam-Bodden is an author and recognized international speaker. Brian has worked as an architect, developer, mentor, and trainer for several Fortune 500 companies. He is the author of *Beginning POJOs: Spring, Hibernate, JBoss and Tapestry* (Apress), and has also coauthored the Apress Java title *Enterprise Java Development on a Budget: Leveraging Java Open Source Technologies*.

Angyne J. Schock-Smith, PMP (Phillipsburg, New Jersey, U.S.)

Angyne J. Schock-Smith, PMP, is the former president and CEO of Arysta Projex, Inc., an independent firm that served the project management community for 10 years. Prior to that time, Angyne served as a practicing project manager across multiple functions, including global network solutions, sales support, customer care, product management and strategic planning, over an 18-year career with AT&T. As of October 1, 2008, she became senior instructional designer for International Institute for Learning's (IIL) Global Learning Solutions, specializing in project/program management and leadership training and consulting services.

Matt Secoske (Omaha, Nebraska, U.S.)

Matt Secoske is principal of Nimblelogic, LLC, a boutique software development company dedicated to making kick-*** web applications. He blogs at *http://mattsecoske.com* and is on Twitter as *@secos*.

Richard Sheridan (Ann Arbor, Michigan, U.S.)

After only two years in business, Rich Sheridan, CEO of Menlo Innovations, became the Forbes "Hire Yourself" cover story for all those choosing entrepreneurship over unemployment. The next year, it was a *Wall Street Journal* article on the unique office Menlo uses for software design and development. Within six years, Menlo had become one of Inc. 500's fastest-growing privately held firms in the U.S. What makes this story truly remarkable is that it occurred against the backdrop of an IT industry that everyone assumed was leaving the U.S. for offshore.

Sheridan's team at Menlo breaks all the rules and, in doing so, produces phenomenal results for its customers. No walls, offices, doors, or cubes—one big open room, à la Edison's original invention factory in Menlo Park, New Jersey. In this noisy, fun atmosphere, Menlo has produced software for all walks of industry, from health care to scientific equipment to high-fashion e-commerce to diesel motor vehicle diagnostics, and many more.

Software developed by Menlo for its clients is designed for everyday people by Menlo's High-tech Anthropologists®, built to last by Menlo's world-class agile software development team, and managed by a set of professional project managers listed among the nation's 50 Most Prolific by the Project Management Institute. Sheridan and Menlo have won numerous awards and honors, and he and his team regularly are invited to present nationally and internationally, sharing the secrets of the Menlo Software Factory™ with all who wish to learn how to build a learning organization that can keep pace with today's advances in software and design.

Derry Simmel, PMP, MBA, FLMI (Chapin, South Carolina, U.S.)

Derry Simmel has been in IT and project management for over 25 years. Recently he has been creating PMOs, having built three in the last six years. The latest of theses is for an $89 million program for the state of South Carolina. Derry has an MBA from the University of Phoenix and a BS in computer science from the University of South Carolina. He currently serves as the vice-chairman of membership for PMI's Project Management Office Specific Interest Group and as the VP of programs for the PMI Midlands Chapter.

Pavel Simsa, PMP (Bellevue, Washington, U.S.)

Pavel Simsa has been in the software development and localization business for 10 years, 5 of which were project and program management of enterprise security software. He works for an international corporation with stakeholders generally spread across the globe for each project. Each product is typically released in 10–17 different languages, all at the same time. Although he earned his PMP® certification only in 2008, he has been following the *PMBOK® Guide* best practices for several years, trying to apply them to the unique, agile, and challenging world of software.

Ken Sipe (St. Charles, Missouri, U.S.)

Ken Sipe is a technology director with Perficient, Inc. (PRFT). Ken was the founder of CodeMentor, where he was the chief architect and mentor, leading clients in the execution of RUP and agile methodologies in the delivery of software solutions. He is a former trainer for Rational in OOAD and RUP, and a CORBA Visibroker trainer for Borland. He continues to enjoy providing training and mentoring in all aspects of software development.

Ken is also a regular speaker with NFJS—No Fluff Just Stuff.

Marty Skomal, MPA (Omaha, Nebraska, U.S.)

Marty Skomal is director of programs at the Nebraska Arts Council, where he supervises all organizational grant programs, including arts education, multicultural arts, and arts touring. He has served as a conference presenter and panelist for numerous state arts agencies, the Kennedy Center for the Performing Arts, and the National Endowment for the Arts. He is also a former NEA Fellowship recipient in the Arts Administration Fellows Program and serves as a national arts program evaluator and consultant.

Marty holds a master's degree in public administration from the University of Nebraska.

Brian Sletten (Beverly Hills, California, U.S.)

Brian Sletten is a liberal arts–educated software engineer with a focus on forward-leaning technologies. He has a background as a system architect, a developer, a mentor, and a trainer. His experience has spanned the online games, defense, finance, and commercial domains with security consulting, network matrix switch controls, 3D simulation/visualization, Grid Computing, P2P, and semantic web–based systems. He has a BS in computer science from the College of William and Mary and currently lives in Beverly Hills, California. He is a senior platform engineer for Riot Games in Culver City, California, working on *League of Legends*. He focuses on web architecture, resource-oriented computing, the semantic web, scalable systems, and security consulting.

Venkat Subramaniam (Broomfield, Colorado, U.S.)

Venkat Subramaniam, founder of Agile Developer, Inc., has trained and mentored thousands of software developers in the U.S., Canada, Europe, and Asia. He helps his clients succeed with agile development and various software technologies.

Venkat is a frequently invited speaker at various international software conferences. He authored *.NET Gotchas* (O'Reilly), and coauthored the 2007 Jolt Productivity Award–winning book *Practices of an Agile Developer* (Pragmatic Bookshelf). His most recent book is *Programming Groovy* (also Pragmatic).

You can reach him at *venkats@agiledeveloper.com*.

Miyoko Takeya, PMP (Tokyo, Japan)

Miyoko Takeya is a member of the Project Management Institute (PMI), the Project Management Association Japan (PMAJ), and the Japan Software Engineering and Management Society (SEMS).

For more than 30 years, she has worked in the information technology industry in Japan, starting with Hitachi Co. Ltd. as an operating system programmer, moving to Digital Equipment Co., and then to NCR Japan.

While she was at Digital and NCR, Miyoko spent most of her time on project business and drove several programs for business quality and performance. She also established a PMO (project management office), through which she was able to implement a project management system, a project accounting system, a project pricing system, an activity reporting and tracking system, and many other systems used successfully for business quality and performance improvement.

Miyoko has enjoyed her work in the IT industry project business area a great deal. Currently, she runs her own consulting business for project management.

Fabio Teixeira de Melo, PMP (Coatzacoalcos, Veracruz, Mexico)

Fabio Pereira Teixeira de Melo, PMP, is a planning manager working for Construtora Norberto Odebrecht, the construction arm of the Brazilian multinational Odebrecht Group, with headquarters in Salvador–BA, Brazil, and offices in 15 countries. His experience spans 15 years in construction, including EPC projects in energy, oil, gas, and petrochemical areas. A Leadership Institute Graduate from the 2004 class and founder and former president of PMI Recife, Pernambuco, Brazil Chapter, Fabio participated in the elaboration of the Construction Extension to the *PMBOK® Guide* and the Practice Standard for Scheduling®, and served a five-year term as Latin America chair for the DPC SIG.

Luis E. Torres, PMP (San Rafael, Alajuela, Costa Rica)

Luis E. Torres is a PMP® certified by the Project Management Institute (PMI). He holds a master's degree in project management (Universitat Ramon Llull, Barcelona, Spain), MBAs in banking and finance (University of Costa Rica) and international business (University of Costa Rica – National University, San Diego, California), and a Licentiate in Mechanical Engineering (University of Costa Rica). Luis has over 15 years of combined experience in the fields of strategic planning and budgeting, project management and financial analysis for multinational companies, administration of international procurement contracts, and project engineering.

Harry Tucker (Matawan, New Jersey, U.S.)

Harry Tucker (*http://www.harrytucker.com*) is consumed by excellence in leadership incubation, collaboration, and personal empowerment. He believes that current social, political, and ecological conditions warrant a sense of urgency to incubate these leadership attributes in others. To that point, he and his associates work with recognized leaders in personal empowerment and leadership development to incubate skills and knowledge in others while igniting their passion to make effective contributions to the world.

Harry currently serves as a leadership incubator and strategy advisor to Fortune 100 companies and has served Wall Street clients for almost 20 years. Previously, Harry worked as an award-winning senior enterprise strategy advisor and architect with Microsoft. He is the founder of the Microsoft Personal Empowerment Group, a private group within Microsoft dedicated to incubating the growth of personal and professional success. In 2005, Harry also incubated a goal-setting and life-architecture program for inner-city youth.

In addition to enjoying life with his partner Rowan and three wonderful kids, Harry enjoys fly-fishing and reading, writing, studying, speaking, and breathing personal empowerment principles.

Lorin Unger (Hoboken, New Jersey, U.S.)

Lorin Unger has over 12 years of experience in technology strategy and management in environments ranging from dot-com to finance.

His specialties include technical strategy, team building and management, process creation and implementation, offshore development procedure implementation and management, efficiency analysis, and patience.

Angelo Valle (Rio de Janeiro, Brazil)

Angelo Valle is a specialist in technological innovation and industry organization civil engineer, master in construction management, at Federal University, Rio de Janeiro, Brazil. He is the immediate past president of the Rio de Janeiro Project Management Institute (PMI) chapter.

Angelo is a noted author of numerous papers. His latest areas of interest revolve around project management organizations (PMOs) and earned value. As academic coordinator of the MBA for Foundation Getulio Vargas, he is currently responsible for the education of more than 20,000 postgraduate students.

Lelio Varella, PMP (Tijuca, Rio de Janeiro, Brazil)

Lelio Varella is a business management consultant with over 30 years of experience and a focus on strategic planning and organizational development; portfolio, program, and project management; and project management offices. He has provided service for some of the most important Brazilian companies in sectors spreading from IT to oil and gas. A skilled spokesperson and instructor, he has coauthored or participated in three project management books. Lelio has been an active volunteer for PMI for more than 10 years, and his achievements include founding the PMI Rio de Janeiro chapter, which currently has over 1,000 members.

Paul Waggoner, MBA, PMP, MCSE, CHP, CHSS (Waukee, Iowa, U.S.)

Paul Waggoner, MBA, PMP, MCSE, CHP, CHSS, is an independent consultant and contract project manager. Paul has over 20 years of experience working in healthcare, information technology, and security. As a healthcare specialist, he works in the provider as well as payer environments.

For the past 10 years, Paul has worked as a project manager helping establish a PMO and completing a wide range of systems and clinical projects. He has also held several technical and management positions and worked as a director of a large information systems department in the midwest. He also co-owned a computer training business and performed a wide range of technical and administrative responsibilities.

Adrian Wible (New York, New York, U.S.)

Adrian Wible's self-chosen title is "Software Development Catalyst"; he works for ThoughtWorks, Inc., mostly in project management roles, but strives to fend off suggestions of being "post-technical" by getting his hands dirty in software development from time to time. He was indoctrinated in the Waterfall/SDLC mode of development as a developer at IBM, and moved into project, people, and process management roles throughout his 20+ year career there and at Dell Computer Corporation. Adrian joined ThoughtWorks and discovered the Agile Manifesto (and XP, and Scrum, and…) in 2005, and realized that project work and management *could* be fun, exciting, and rewarding. He hasn't looked back since.

Adrian can be reached at *awible@thoughtworks.com*.

David Wood (Fredericksburg, Virginia, U.S.)

David Wood is a partner of Zepheira, where he manages software projects and recommends the application of disruptive technologies to maximize business opportunities.

David has been involved with the development of semantic web standards, tools, products, and services since 1999. He cochaired the Semantic Web Best Practices and Deployment Working Group at the W3C, and was a member of the Semantic Web Coordination Group. He is a founding member of several open source software projects, including the Kowari Metastore, the Mulgara Semantic Store, and the recently rearchitected Persistent URL service.

Most recently, David was entrepreneur-in-residence at the MIND Laboratory within the University of Maryland Institute for Advanced Computer Studies. He lead the implementation team for the Policy-Aware Web project, which developed a next-generation access-control system for the World Wide Web. David founded Tucana Technologies, Inc., a purveyor of a semantic web database purchased by Northrop Grumman Corporation in 2005. Prior to Tucana, David founded Plugged In Software, a successful software services firm in Australia from 1995–2002.

David is an adjunct instructor of computer science at the University of Mary Washington and researches the application of recombinant data techniques to software maintenance at the University of Queensland.

Joe Zenevitch (New York, New York, U.S.)

Joe Zenevitch is a senior project manager with ThoughtWorks, Inc., where he provides program and project management services for state-of-the-art software development projects, in addition to business analysis and agile coaching. Joe has over 20 years of experience in software development, with the past 15 focused on project management. While he has background in traditional project management methods, he has specialized in agile project management since ThoughtWorks began adopting it on projects in 1998.

Joe can be reached at *joez@thoughtworks.com*.

Index

Colophon

The cover and heading font is Gotham; the text font is Minion Pro.

Related Titles from O'Reilly

Software Development

Applied Software Project Management

Beautiful Code

Designing Interfaces

Essential Business Process Modeling

Enterprise Service Bus

Head First Design Patterns

Head First Design Patterns Poster

Head First Object-Oriented Analysis and Design

Head First PMP

Head First Software Development

Learning UML 2.0

Masterminds of Programming

Practical Development Environments

Prefactoring

Process Improvement Essentials

SOA in Practice

The Art of Agile Development

UML 2.0 in a Nutshell

UML 2.0 Pocket Reference

O'REILLY®

Our books are available at most retail and online bookstores.

To order direct: 1-800-998-9938 • *order@oreilly.com* • *www.oreilly.com*

Online editions of most O'Reilly titles are available by subscription at *safari.oreilly.com*